Defenseless Christianity

Published in association with
Bluffton University

Defenseless Christianity

Anabaptism for a Nonviolent Church

Gerald J. Mast
J. Denny Weaver

Foreword by Greg Boyd

Cascadia
Publishing House
Telford, Pennsylvania

copublished with
Herald Press
Scottdale, Pennsylvania

Cascadia Publishing House LLC orders, information, reprint permissions:
contact@cascadiapublishinghouse.com
1-215-723-9125
126 Klingerman Road, Telford PA 18969
www.CascadiaPublishingHouse.com

Defenseless Christianity
Copyright © 2009 by Cascadia Publishing House
a division of Cascadia Publishing House LLC, Telford, PA 18969
All rights reserved.
Copublished with Herald Press, Scottdale, PA
Library of Congress Catalog Number: 2009019254
ISBN 13: 978-1-931038-63-8 **ISBN 10:** 1-931038-63-5
Book design by Cascadia Publishing House
Cover design by Merrill R. Miller

Library of Congress Cataloguing-in-Publication Data
Mast, Gerald J., 1965-
  Defenseless Christianity : Anabaptism for a nonviolent church / Gerald J.
Mast and J. Denny Weaver ; foreword by Greg Boyd.
     p. cm.
  Summary: "Proposing an Anabaptism defined as defenseless Christianity,
the authors contend it should be seen as a nonviolent Christian movement
with a world-reconciling theology even though some first-generation Ana-
baptists were not pacifists." "[summary]"--Provided by publisher.
  Includes bibliographical references (p.   ) and index.
  ISBN-13: 978-1-931038-63-8 (5.5 x 8.5" trade pbk. : alk. paper)
  ISBN-10: 1-931038-63-5 (5.5 x 8.5" trade pbk. : alk. paper)
  1. Anabaptists. 2. Anabaptists--Doctrines. 3. Nonviolence--Religious as-
pects--Anabaptists. 4. Nonviolence--Religious aspects--Christianity. I.
Weaver, J. Denny, 1941- II. Title.

BX4931.3.M37 2009
261.8'73--dc22

2009019254

16 15 13 12 11 10 09   10 9 8 7 6 5 4 3 2 1

*To the memory of C. Henry Smith,
teacher and writer of Mennonite history,
who believed that "The Mennonite church,
if she wishes to be useful in the world, must respect
herself and the faith she represents."*

Contents

Foreword

JESUS TAUGHT US to be peacemakers, to love and serve our enemies, and to never resort to violence, even in self-defense. One might have thought this would incline Christians to have a rather unfavorable view of torture. It doesn't, at least not in America. A study by the Pew Forum on Religion and Public Life actually found that Christians tend to have a significantly more favorable view of torture than others.

Tragically, this research is hardly surprising. Throughout history the church has more often than not allowed itself to be co-opted by nationalistic agendas and has given its support to "justified" violence. Indeed, in the name of the one who laid down his life for his enemies, the church has often led the battle cry to torture and kill them.

At the same time, one thankfully finds throughout history individuals and movements who remained faithful to Christ by choosing the way of the cross over the way of the sword. In the modern period, the clearest expression of this resistance to the violent-prone "church militant and triumphant" has been the Anabaptist movement. As Weaver and Mast show in this historically insightful and theologically relevant book, the Anabaptist movement was centered on the New Testament's call to follow Jesus' loving example of remaining defenseless rather than resorting to violence.

While the call to love enemies and refuse violence looks foolish to people whose minds have been conditioned by violence, it is for just this reason the clearest witness to the beauty of a kingdom that is "not of this world." One need not agree with each specific proposal Weaver and Mast make in this book regarding various ways of engaging government on issues of violence to appreciate the beauty and importance of the defenseless, Christlike lifestyle itself.

As the Pew poll revealed, the church today continues to significantly conform to the common sense of our violent-prone world. Sadly, even some within the Anabaptist tradition are backing away from the scandalous beauty of a commitment to nonviolence. At the same time, there are multitudes of individuals and movements scattered throughout the world who are discovering the centrality of this beautiful foolishness and who are looking for an ecclesial tradition to call home. In this light, the historical exposition of the theme of nonviolence found in *Defenseless Christianity* could not be more timely.

My hope is that God uses this book to call Anabaptists along with other Jesus-followers back to the beautifully foolish, enemy-loving, cross-bearing center of our faith.

—*Greg Boyd, St. Paul, Minnesota*
Author, The Myth of a Christian Nation; *Pastor, Woodland Hills Church; and Adjunct Professor; Bethel University, St. Paul.*

Authors' Preface

THIS SMALL BOOK HAS BOTH A PARTICULAR and an abiding genesis. The particular genesis, that which precipitated the initial draft of the book, was the existence of the Anabaptist Seminar following the Anabaptist Colloquium that met at Eastern Mennonite University in April 2006. The assignment for the presenters at the seminar was to discuss the relevance for the contemporary church of their findings presented in the history-focused colloquium. The invitation to the seminar constituted the specific impetus to put in writing the abiding genesis of our work, namely our ongoing, longstanding, many-sided discussions about the character of sixteenth-century Anabaptism and its importance for the contemporary church.

This book was thus actually begun long before either of us knew we were writing a book together. It has been a mutually enriching conversation. We have grown through dealing with our differing academic disciplines: theology and rhetoric. It is our intent that the book display that mutual learning.

Alongside our ongoing conversations, producing the actual manuscript for the book was also a cooperative activity. Each of us wrote first drafts of some sections, and the other author then revised and expanded the draft. Each author has worked over the entire manuscript so that both of us identify with the whole.

We have together shaped what some may read as a polemical tract. Indeed our project has a polemical edge and should be evaluated both as a sober work of scholarship and as a passionate advocacy of defenseless Christianity. There is urgency here. We advocate our perspectives and oppose other understandings.

Some may discern a contradiction between "defenseless" Christianity and our vigorous arguments. However, defenseless Christianity as we understand it has always been a contentious, quarrelsome discursive community. For example, the peaceable images of the lamb and the sun on this book's cover are drawn from the emblems of two sides in a "War of the Lambs" seventeenth-century Dutch Mennonite controversy. Our own habits of writing are at times shaped more by the argumentative testimonies found in early Anabaptist source texts than by proper academic or theological writing. Such Anabaptist argument may arise from unwillingness to go farther than speaking or writing in the effort to persuade. Mild speech could be a luxury for those in charge or having the most weapons, hence the maxim, "speak softly and carry a big stick." We do not speak softly in urging Christianity to give up the big stick it has too often wielded. Nevertheless, if our quest to draw contrasts seems unfair to some viewpoints, we expect vigorous arguments to provoke vigorous critique, in trust that such exchanges can enlarge rather than diminish a defenseless Christian vision.

We are grateful to our colleagues from around the world who debate the character of Anabaptism. Even when we disagree with some of their views, the conversation keeps interest in Anabaptism alive and also demonstrates its importance for the future of the peace churches. We are grateful to publisher Michael A. King for his interest and support of this manuscript in particular and for his important work of managing Cascadia Publishing House LLC to give visibility to Anabaptist-oriented publications generally. And we are grateful to Bluffton University: for bringing us together in the mission of Anabaptist education; for providing an institutional context that is supportive of the time and energy required to address the kinds of questions we take up in this book; and for generous financial support for publication of the manuscript. The index was prepared by Anna Yoder, a Bluffton University student and now a veteran indexer in her role as the research assistant for the Communication and Theatre Department.

C. Henry Smith, who taught at Bluffton University during the first half of the twentieth century, had much to do with beginning the recovery of the Anabaptist Vision, even though he was party to significant disagreements about how to interpret Anabaptist-Mennonite history. His work helped the Mennonite church remember its Anabaptist roots and to begin thinking critically about how to continue the Anabaptist witness today. Grateful for his legacy, we dedicate this work to his memory.

—*Gerald J. Mast, Bluffton University*
  J. Denny Weaver, Bluffton University

Defenseless Christianity

Chapter 1

Defenseless Christianity as New Creation

ONE OF THE DISCOVERIES OF NEW TESTAMENT SCHOLARSHIP in the twentieth century was the communal and social character of the apostle Paul's view of salvation. Partly due to Luther's long shadow of influence, Protestant Christians had for centuries understood the work of Jesus Christ to be primarily the achievement of a personal relationship to God that changes an individual's self-understanding and motivation.

Through the work of Oscar Cullman, Krister Stendahl, E. P. Sanders, Paul Minear, and others, it became clear that Paul's apostolic witness was not only that the life, death, and resurrection of Jesus changed individuals' status before God, but also that through Jesus Christ God is bringing about a new world, a new society, a new kind of human relationship, based on peace and reconciliation rather than on fear and antagonism. This discovery was made visible more broadly through the widespread reception of John Howard Yoder's book *The Politics of Jesus*, in which it is argued that the life of Jesus Christ is a model and an empowerment for a renewed and reconciled society that challenges the warring habits of the present order.

PEACE AS THE GOSPEL

One key aspect of this reconciled relationship made possible in Jesus Christ is, of course, defenselessness. Yoder stated it most clearly in the eleventh chapter of *The Politics of Jesus*, when he described the full meaning of justification in the following way: "It is the good news that my enemy and I are united, through no merit or work of our own, in a new humanity that forbids henceforth my ever taking his or her life in my hands."[1] We can think of no better way to articulate the centrality of peace to the gospel of Jesus Christ, and we seek in this short book to explain the contribution we believe Anabaptist history and theology can make toward the recognition that the work of Jesus Christ and his church is essentially the work of peace and reconciliation—between God and humans first of all, and then among divided and violence-prone human beings of every race and tribe and across gender lines.

We are thus unapologetic about the prominent place given to peace in our account of Anabaptist Christianity. The historical grounds for this prominence are made clear in Chapter 2. But here we want to also address a theological objection that often arises to such a presentation of the gospel. Is not the emphasis on peace a reduction of the gospel to a merely political or social end? Is not the gospel of Jesus Christ deeper and broader than our narrow preoccupation with war and violence?

We believe that such an accusation can only arise from an insidious and long-established ideological habit whereby the gospel is first of all reduced to an essence that is presumed to be before its social visibility: spiritual vitality, the salvation of souls, the satisfaction of God's wrath, or some other such abstract or invisible aspect. From the standpoint of such an assumption, we are then accused of making central what should be properly peripheral. The important thing, we are told, is the salvation of souls, not our response to violence and social injustice. The important thing is getting right with God, we hear, and we ought not hamper seekers by arguing about the form of relationships that Christians should have with one another across national, racial, sexual, or other boundary lines. Others will agree with us that it is important to pursue peace, but only after first being converted or having a relationship with God.

We submit that the good news of the gospel is as concrete and specific at its core as the resurrection of our very bodies and reconciliation with our enemies. This resurrection-based form of reconciliation with God and our neighbors has been accomplished by the life and body of Jesus Christ, a reconciliation not observed by the vast majority of the world's people, who remain blind to the work of God in Jesus Christ. However, for believers with eyes to see, the amazing good news of the gospel is the visible tearing down of all walls that divide us from our neighbors—and the establishment of a new humanity that is at peace with God and one another. Because of this new creation that Jesus Christ announces in his life, death, and resurrection, we are freed to love God and our neighbors without reserve. Jesus Christ has saved us from all of the falsehood and mistrust, anger and malice, jealousy and hatred, from all of the sinful preoccupations and bondages that separate us from God's good creation in us and around us.

Moreover, we are convinced that the most profound truth of Christianity is also the most neglected feature of really existing Christianity. The way of Jesus Christ is the way of peace. In peaceful service to others, Jesus became Lord of the universe. Thus, our peaceful and peacemaking service to others is the work of God—in line with the grain of the universe, a witness to the truth that makes us free, a present foretaste of the future reign of God. For us, this gospel of peace is not reductionist; rather, this biblical whole gospel vision has even more good news in it than the stripped-down story told by the classic creeds and the "orthodoxy" that has been based on such creeds. In other words, we advocate believing "more" than orthodoxy, not less.

NEWNESS AS GOOD NEWS

We wish to highlight a second dimension of the reconciled relationships adding up to a transformed society envisioned by Paul's apostolic witness. The work of Jesus Christ in history and in the church is a new thing that God is doing, and this newness is a defining dimension of that work. Indeed, where Protestants had traditionally read Paul in 2 Corinthians 5:17 to be claiming that "if anyone is in Christ, he is a new creature," (as the King James Version has it, as well as the RSV and NIV), we now understand, as more recent translations put it, that Paul was saying "in Christ, there is a new creation" (NRSV), that "in Christ, the new creation has come" (TNIV).

This "new" discovery in biblical studies strengthens our understanding of the comprehensive newness of the good news of the gospel. For those who are in Christ, the world and our neighbors are no longer regarded from a "human point of view" but from a location and a new perspective made possible by our attachment to Jesus Christ. This perspective is attentive first of all to the eschatological dimension of history and theology: There is novelty associated with the movement of the Holy Spirit, this novelty is recognizable, and this novelty is a mark of the gospel truth that is being made visible. In this way the viewpoint we are advocating here should be understood as biblical rather than confessional or creedal. We are convinced that a key feature of the biblical canon itself is novelty—that it narrates the history of God's relationship to human beings and God's interventions in human history on behalf of God's peace.

Staying close to the biblical story also keeps alive the surplus of meaning associated with Scripture. Especially as we stay true to the Jewish heritage of Christianity, we will not seek to present the truth of the Bible in a manner only accountable to the systematic coherence demanded of Greek philosophy, for example. The biblical record and its reception reveal a history of argumentation and competing perspectives, particularly in the Old Testament, as Walter Brueggmann has noted.[2] Our view is that Jesus as described in the New Testament can best be seen as participating in the ongoing dispute about God's purposes and actions accounted for in the Jewish sacred writings found in the Old Testament. As Christians, we are convinced by Jesus' interpretation of the law and the testimonies found in Scripture.

Moreover, in the discussion about how to understand the work of Jesus Christ, we find Paul and other writers of New Testament epistles to be convincing as well, although we acknowledge that our reading of the New Testament is shaped by the kind of biblical scholarship Yoder cites in *The Politics of Jesus*. In other words, we see the Scriptures as "inspired" and credible precisely because they contain multiple perspectives that invite the taking of a position amid the controversy, rather than seek to exclude every other perspective from consideration.

In taking a position among such competing perspectives, our intent is that our view is shaped first of all by the story of Jesus Christ. Although we respect and stand under the authority of the whole biblical canon, we do not see ourselves trying to develop a position that accounts for and synthesizes every argument or viewpoint found in the Bible.

The closer we stay to this scriptural controversy, even while taking sides in it, the closer we find ourselves to the dynamic power of the Holy Spirit unleashed at Pentecost and still working today. The more we seek to resolve all the apparent contradictions of the Bible into a coherent synthesis or properly worded propositional statements, the more we distance ourselves from the energy and struggle associated with the transformative and challenging work God is doing in the world. We thus see our own proposal as a contingent articulation of a perspective that is not meant to solve all problems or address every exception. It is rather a testimony of our own convictions about the horizon of gospel truth opened up for Christians by Anabaptist teachings and practices.

When we say that Anabaptism offered a new way forward and a new theology, then, we do not mean that Anabaptists invented a completely unprecedented theological paradigm. We mean rather that they offered to their sixteenth-century context a form of biblical reasoning that exceeded the imaginative horizons of contemporary Catholic and Protestant theologizing. By turning to the Scriptures more than to an "orthodox" belief system or a tradition of authoritative teachings, the Anabaptists were able to "discover" biblical forms of obedience and faithfulness that had been obscured by the priorities and preoccupations of Latin Christendom for centuries. Anabaptists came to realize that the gospel is about concretely changed lives more than about correctly conceived ideas. At the same time, because the Anabaptists sought to think and speak and write about God in ways that strengthened faithful lives, such a priority does end up renewing and revising some traditional ideas from which actions are presumed to follow.

We do not therefore think that the extent to which Anabaptists have been or are "orthodox" matters very much. Far more important than whether someone believes God exists is what a person believes God expects. Far more significant than the question of God's nature and form is the question of our allegiance and obedience. In other words, we do not believe that saying "Lord" in the right way matters so much as giving to the Lord in the right way. Put another way, the Anabaptists practiced what Brian McLaren calls a generous orthodoxy, with considerable flexibility for changes in context and circumstances and an appreciation for improvisation that strengthens faithful practices.[3]

We are committed to the biblical testimony that God has a people through whom God has acted and is acting in human history. God has chosen Israel and the church of Jesus Christ to bear the first fruits of the new creation that God is bringing about. A faithful reading of history thus turns an attentive eye to the ways in which God's people have discovered the "new thing" God is doing and have aligned themselves with it. As Rowan Williams has put it with his usual eloquence, "When we examine a past period, we should, then, ask what it was that made it impossible for Christians simply to repeat what had been said; we should look for what was not simply the reflection of cultural attitudes . . . what unsettles the Church, what appears with increasing urgency as unfinished business."[4]

Finally, we do believe that the biblical witness makes visible, amid all of the controversy found there, the direction of God's purposes and methods in the coming of God's peaceable reign. The God of Israel and Jesus Christ is a God of righteousness and forgiveness; of justice and peace. This God is one whose power shatters the spear and breaks the sword. This God is one who defeats violence and war and human brutality of all kinds with fierce and undying love. This God breaks down barriers of class, nationalism, race and gender. The God of Jesus Christ is a God of peace. We seek in the following two chapters to witness to this God.

At the same time, the new creation that we believe God is bringing about also makes us aware of what astute readers will consider a shortcoming of our work. Although we wrote that the new creation tears down barriers of gender and race, we are acutely aware that the conversation partners for this study of historical Anabaptism are male—and that the discipline of Anabaptist studies remains dominated by Caucasian male scholars. While our awareness and treatment of violence issues in chapter 3 is shaped by the work of feminist and African-American writers,[5] we wonder how the discussion of the historical issues themselves might change if more female scholars and scholars of color were in the conversation. It is to be hoped that the rising generation will know the answer.

NOTES

1. John Howard Yoder, *The Politics of Jesus: Vicit Agnus Noster*, 2nd. ed. (Grand Rapids, Mich.: William B. Eerdmans, 1993), 226.

2. Walter Brueggemann, *The Theology of the Old Testament: Testimony, Dispute, Advocacy* (Minneapolis: Fortress Press, 1997), 108-14.

3. "Generous orthodoxy . . . affirms . . . that Scripture itself remains above the creeds and that the Holy Spirit may use Scripture to tweak our creedal understandings and emphases from time to time, so that new creeds are needed to give voice to the cry of faith today." Brian D. McLaren, *A Generous Orthodoxy: Why I Am a Missional, Evangelical, Post-Protestant, Liberal/Conservative, Mystical/Poetic, Biblical, Charismatic/Contemplative, Fundamentalist/Calvinist, Anabaptist/Anglican, Methodist, Catholic, Green, Incarnational, Depressed-Yet-Hopeful, Emergent, Unfinished Christian* (Grand Rapids, Mich.: Zondervan, 2004), 28.

4. Rowan Williams, *Why Study the Past? The Quest for the Historical Church* (Grand Rapids, Mich.: William B. Eerdmans Publishing Company, 2005), 97.

5. Representative, seminal literature includes Rita Nakashima Brock and Rebecca Ann Parker, *Saving Paradise: How Christianity Traded Love of This World for Crucifixion and Empire* (Boston: Beacon Press, 2008); Rita Nakashima Brock, *Journeys by Heart: A Christology of Erotic Power* (New York: Crossroad, 1991); Joanne Carlson Brown and Carole R. Bohn, eds., *Christianity, Patriarchy, and Abuse: A Feminist Critique* (New York: The Pilgrim Press, 1989); James H. Cone, *God of the Oppressed*, rev. ed. (Maryknoll, N.Y.: Orbis Books, 1997); Rosemary Radford Ruether, *Sexism and God-talk: Toward a Feminist Theology* (Boston: Beacon Press, 1983); Susan Brooks Thistlethwaite, *Sex, Race and God: Christian Feminism in Black and White* (New York: Crossroad, 1991); Delores S. Williams, *Sisters in the Wilderness: The Challenge of Womanist God-Talk* (Maryknoll, N.Y.: Orbis Books, 1993).

Chapter 3

Defenseless Christianity in the Radical Reformation

IN THE RESONANT WORDS OF KING JAMES ENGLISH, "Where there is no vision, the people perish" (Prov. 29.18). This chapter presents an account of sixteenth-century Anabaptist history as a "vision" for the church rooted in the Word of God, the resurrection of Jesus Christ, and God's peaceable reign, which was only partly fulfilled in the various Anabaptist movements shaped by that vision.

History comes alive when a story is told that links people and events into a larger narrative with meaning for the present. We believe that the story of sixteenth-century Anabaptism is such a narrative—a living tradition with meaning for the present and future church.[1] While this chapter focuses on the distinctive vision that shaped Anabaptist historical movements, the next chapter will offer defenseless Anabaptism as a living tradition for contemporary Christians and the church of the twenty-first century.[2]

Anabaptism of the vision we present can be designated with two names, one contemporary and one historical. Using contemporary language borrowed from the academy, we call it *nonviolent ecclesial Anabaptism*. The term *nonviolent* distinguishes this Anabaptism from versions of Anabaptism that espoused the sword, although as our discussion below indicates, we are not denying the sword-bearers their identification as Anabaptists nor omitting them from the historical narrative. The term *ecclesial* indicates that Anabaptism as we understand it is first of all a persuasive understanding of the church that was new and distinct in the early sixteenth century.

Second, our vision of Anabaptism carries the designation of *defenseless Christianity*. This name has historical precedent. It comes from the complete title of *Martyrs Mirror*, which begins *The Bloody Theater or Martyrs Mirror of the Defenseless Christians*.[3] Use of this designation links our vision of Anabaptism to terminology used by Anabaptists themselves.

Beyond this historical precedent, the reference to defenseless *Christians* makes clear that we are talking about a vision applicable to all Christians. This name makes clear that the Anabaptist narrative is a story that links the believer, whether sixteenth-century or contemporary, to Jesus Christ. More particularly, the name makes visible the fact that the rejection of violence is not a peculiar privilege of nor a special pleading by the peace churches. Peace is the will of God and is of a piece with the grain of the universe, as John Howard Yoder has said.[4] In other words, peace in general and defenselessness in particular have their most profound source in Jesus Christ, his cross and resurrection. As such it is a challenge to every person who professes faith in Jesus. The good news about Jesus Christ is the gospel of peace. And Anabaptism is meaningful as a vision because it links this gospel to the historic and contemporary church.

The vision we present has something to say to all groups across the spectrum of Mennonites, Amish, Brethren, and other lineal descendants of sixteenth-century Anabaptism as well as to Anabaptists in denominations not usually associated with Anabaptists. Although we write from the standpoint of the culturally assimilated Mennonite Church USA, it is possible that our vision is relevant for the conservative side of the twenty-first century Anabaptist spectrum, especially those conservative Mennonites, Amish, and Brethren who are struggling with the attractions of nationalism, fundamentalism, individualism, and consumerism. In that struggle, our vision of Anabaptism unabashedly supports nonconformity to popular forms of Christianity that reduce faith to an inner experience without expecting visible difference from the "world." Further, our multifaceted approach to Anabaptism, which explains why there can be no uncontested normative version of the vision, can lend support to various conservative versions of Anabaptism seeking a theological basis for a nonconformist witness based in biblical humility rather than militant fundamentalism.

At the same time, our vision speaks to the so-called progressive Mennonite conferences, as well as to Brethren and other lineal descendants of sixteenth-century Anabaptism. In a variety of conversations, these culturally progressive denominations are asking what it means to be Mennonite or Anabaptist or a "peace church." Our vision seems particularly apt for Mennonite Church USA, in which our own churchly roots are nourished. At its biennial convention in San Jose, California (July 2007) it passed a resolution to explore the denomination's "national identity" as people living in "what many consider to be the wealthiest and most powerful nation on Earth," and requesting resources to aid in living "faithfully in Christ-like ways, sometimes at odds with our national culture, acknowledging that no culture is either completely redeemed or completely fallen."[5]

The conversations about the shape of the church for these contemporary progressive descendants of Anabaptism take many forms. Some debate whether to drop the designation *Mennonite* from the name of congregations or conferences. There are conversations about what it means to be missional or evangelical, whether the message of peace and nonviolence hinders mission outreach, whether nonviolence is part of the missional gospel, whether the contemporary church is too much identified with the social order or is rather irresponsible in not being more involved in governing the social order. The several Brethren denominations carry on their own version of these conversations. Our vision of Anabaptism as defenseless Christianity seeks to contribute to all these conversations.

Just as importantly, the vision presented in this essay speaks to Anabaptists living and serving among denominations that do not stand in the line of lineal descendants from sixteenth-century Anabaptism. We encounter these folks in increasing numbers in our interactions in both academic and churchly settings in groups not usually thought of as Anabaptists. We have represented Anabaptist perspectives in a variety of settings and have received positive responses and support from Catholics, Methodists, Presbyterians, Anglicans, ecumenical groupings, Evangelicals, and others. Some of these Anabaptists belong to the Anabaptist Association of Australia and New Zealand, which links like-minded believers scattered across these countries. Others belong to a similar network that exists in the United Kingdom.

When Weaver spoke several years ago on the subject of nonviolence and theology to the Anabaptist Seminar in London, which attracts participants from all over England, one man responded, "I belong to the Anglican parish at _____, but I want you to know that I am an Anabaptist." When Mast attended a gathering of Mennonite denominational boards, he encountered Greg Boyd, who famously divided his Baptist mega-church congregation in St. Paul by preaching that the gospel of Jesus Christ is distinguished from the nationalistic and militaristic ideology of American patriotism. Boyd told Mennonite leaders that he and others like him are looking for a tradition of witness to the gospel of peace, which he has discovered in Anabaptism. The vision of Anabaptism as defenseless Christianity is an offering for all such seekers of the Jesus way of peace, as well as for our sisters and brothers in the Mennonite churches and other Anabaptist communions.

To offer a characterization of sixteenth-century Anabaptism and to suggest its meaning and significance for the contemporary church is to enter disputed territory. This chapter and the one to follow enter that territory in two steps. For us, the defenseless Christianity of nonviolent ecclesial Anabaptism is best defined as a movement of Christian conviction and action that gathered baptized believers into peaceable charismatic communities organized by the rule of Christ and identified with the peaceable reign of God. This chapter develops our framework for understanding this form of Anabaptism as a historical movement in the sixteenth century. The next chapter uses the historical analysis to recognize defenseless Christianity as a contemporary, ongoing phenomenon, a living tradition that still shapes the way we live in the world as Christians in the twenty-first century.

The project draws from but also extends arguments found in our recent publications on Anabaptism, including Mast's *Separation and the Sword in Anabaptist Persuasion*, Weaver's revised edition of *Becoming Anabaptist*, and our jointly edited *Teaching Peace*.[6] Along with those complementary publications, however, our longtime and ongoing discussions have led to a vision of defenseless Christianity, past and present, shaped by spirit-guided persuasion more than by systematic or orthodox theology. Our different disciplinary locations in communication and theology are thus brought together in our understanding of Anabaptist persuasion—a theology for faithful and peaceful living.

Offering a perspective on sixteenth-century Anabaptism is, of course, an activity with significant recent precedents. Harold S. Bender's "Anabaptist Vision," which originated as his 1943 presidential address to the American Society of Church History,[7] served as the operative historical paradigm of Anabaptism into the 1970s and still functions as a reference point even for those scholars who dispute Bender's paradigm and claim to be "beyond" it. In the 1970s, Bender's thesis of Anabaptism as a homogeneous movement that began from a single source in Zurich, Switzerland gave way to the paradigm of "polygenesis." According to this paradigm, whose common designation came from an article title, "From Monogenesis to Polygenesis," Anabaptism had several independent points of origin which quite naturally produced a pluralistic movement.[8]

Our approach owes something both to Bender's "Anabaptist Vision" and to the polygenesis proposal, but is neither a fusion of the two nor a middle point between them. It seeks instead to find in Anabaptism that which can be seen as the "new" thing God was doing in that early modern time and place. This perspective is consistent with a well-known early Anabaptist text—the Schleitheim *Brotherly Union*—which emphasizes the unity that was discovered and made known through Spirit-guided searching of the Scriptures, a renewed knowledge that needed to be fulfilled in the lives of those who were committed to "standing fast."

Our perspective has also been shaped by a learning from what is sometimes called postmodernity, namely that a neutral historical account does not exist and that every historical telling then reflects a particular vantage point. Thus posing an alternative either to Bender's presentation of "The Anabaptist Vision" or to the polygenesis paradigm is not to claim supersession on the basis of the truth or falsehood of these historical postures. It is, rather, to suggest other, more persuasive and useful ways of looking at the meaning of the data of history.

In connection with postmodernity, we are convinced the discipline of rhetoric sheds useful light on Anabaptist texts. Rhetorical criticism reads texts not so much as static entities containing fixed truth claims but as living statements functioning as tactical assertions in a context whose contours are subject to change.[9] The result of this analysis describes Anabaptism not in terms of a distilled essence but as a dynamic movement, shaped by assumptions recognizably close to Bender's original Anabaptist Vision but existing in multiple versions of charismatic Christian communities shaped by the narrative of Jesus and living according to his rejection of the sword, while responding to the changing actions of civil and religious authorities who opposed such practices.

Thus Anabaptism did not rest on some underlying essence that was shared with Christendom or among its own varied expressions. Anabaptism is instead an irruption in Christendom, a symptom of Christendom's own unsustainable contradictions as they were experienced in early modernity.

At the same time, we are prepared to interpret Anabaptism in a way consistent with the self-understanding of many early Anabaptists. They believed that their communities were the result of the movement of the Holy Spirit, of the discovery anew of the way and rule of Jesus Christ, and of the inexplicable power of the Word of God.

Ours is not the only effort to pose a post-polygenesis paradigm. Our paradigm appears alongside Arnold Snyder's effort to develop a description of Anabaptism that includes most characters and groups called "Anabaptist" except for the anti-trinitarians, and then to define the theological paradigm of Anabaptism in terms of a theological core present at the beginning of and visible within all Anabaptist movements as they developed over time and across changing contexts.

Our difference with this effort, as also with Bender and with polygenesis, will become apparent in the presentation of our paradigm for nonviolent ecclesial Anabaptism as defenseless Christianity. Yet, while we see our project as differing from Snyder's, we also share with him a concern to understand Anabaptism as a movement of the church and of the Holy Spirit, whose significance and identity in the sixteenth-century transcended the multiple locations and circumstances of its appearance.[10] We agree with Snyder that Anabaptism is more than the sum of its parts, and we seek with him to understand Anabaptism's development over time.[11]

Our proposal centers on ecclesiology, defining Anabaptism first of all as a distinctive way to be the church in the sixteenth century.[12] It comes into view as the ecclesiology that rejects the idea of a Christian society and the state or territorial church that encompasses that society. That which constitutes the basis of this ecclesiology and shapes its distinction from the social order is the commitment to live out of the story and resurrection of Jesus Christ without defending that commitment through actual or threatened violence; to be, as the letter of the Zurich radicals to Thomas Müntzer put it, "sheep among wolves, sheep for the slaughter."[13] One could call this a first glimpse of Anabaptism as defenseless Christianity. In Bender's "Anabaptist Vision," this impulse was identified as discipleship—*nachfolge Christi.*

Developing as part of the commitment to discipleship is the rejection of the sword and of violence, which is intrinsic to the life and work of Jesus. Other characteristics of Anabaptism, as we understand it, are improvisations that arise from a commitment to this Christ-centered defenseless ecclesiology. As a new way to be the church in the sixteenth-century—that is, as a fresh movement of God identified with the "new creation"—it has the potential to touch all aspects of life and thought.

At first glance, this paradigm may sound like a warmed-over version of Bender. While we are inspired by Bender's version of Anabaptism, we are not simply repeating it. An important part of our description of nonviolent ecclesial Anabaptism is that it cannot be reduced to three seminal points of ecclesiology, discipleship, and nonviolence. While motifs like these clearly shaped the movement, they were articulated in many and multiple ways without an obvious normative form.

Our proposal is also distinguished from a variety of other efforts to characterize Anabaptist essences. We do not think of Anabaptism as an amalgam of themes gathered from disparate sources, nor simply as the sum total of all sixteenth-century Anabaptist movements. Nor is it a hybrid consisting of some Catholic and some Protestant components. Nor a new, simplified version of a medieval movement such as mysticism or monasticism. Nor a way station or a middle point between other groups.

Anabaptism is rather a distinct movement, not without antecedents or earlier precedents of course, but nonetheless a distinct sixteenth-century movement with its own way of being the church—independent of civil authorities, separated from the state church, and separated from the social order. But we should be clear, as was noted in Chapter 1, that we do not understand Anabaptism's distinctiveness as some kind of modern achievement of originality or progress. Since we write from a Christian perspective, we are convinced that Anabaptists were distinctive insofar as they were radically obedient to the way of Jesus Christ and followed the leading of the Holy Spirit amid the particular historical and cultural vagaries of the sixteenth century. In this sense, we are arguing that Anabaptism is best understand not only as a new way to be the church but also as a renewal of the church through a radical stewardship of the gospel.

It is important to state that the Anabaptism(s) described from the vantage point of the defenseless Christianity we are identified with were not simply the product of a singular early vision, although visions and dreams certainly did play a role in the formation of Anabaptist communities. There was not a clearly definable Anabaptism that developed tidily when or because Conrad Grebel and Felix Mantz or Michael Sattler or Pilgram Marpeck or Jacob Hutter or Menno Simons read the Bible and in response proposed an original theological paradigm that was then actualized through a plan of action.

Anabaptism as we are describing it was a product of several kinds of reforming efforts, many of which did involve reading the Bible with renewed understanding in some way that challenged aspects of the social order or the state church or both. Out of these efforts, as leaders variously sought to take the Bible and Christian faith seriously, there emerged different Anabaptist visions and movements that can be loosely characterized in terms of what we have called nonviolent ecclesial Anabaptism—defenseless contrast communities who were empowered by the Holy Spirit to follow Jesus Christ in life.

When applied to sixteenth-century texts, the discipline of rhetoric has proved helpful in understanding the sixteenth-century stories and in developing the interpretative framework from which nonviolent ecclesial Anabaptism becomes visible as a movement. In particular, the discipline of rhetoric clarifies how a controversial conviction—such as rejection of the sword—can help form a movement even though not all adherents accept that conviction. Among early Anabaptists, and even more so among later Anabaptists, rejection of the sword became one point of debate and discussion that distinguished Anabaptist Christians from their Catholic and Reformed neighbors, who were not engaged in that kind of debate among themselves and who were typically opposed to the gradually emerging Anabaptist consensus against accepting the sword of defense or governance as a valid Christian responsibility.

Rhetorical analysis also clarifies how it is that *separation* is not a stance of social withdrawal, as it has been frequently depicted, but actually one of involvement and engagement with the world. For most early Anabaptists who sought to be separated from the surrounding social consensus, separation was a tactic for making the faithful church visible to their neighbors—rather than a practice of quietism.

The first section to follow focuses on the historical development of the ecclesiology of nonviolent Anabaptism. The second section describes several Anabaptists' own statements of this new ecclesiology. The third section illustrates the way that this new ecclesiology set in motion new or renewed theological directions and initiatives. The final section then brings the discipline of rhetorical analysis explicitly to bear on the sixteenth-century materials to show the function of separation and how rejection of the sword (pacifism or defenselessness) could become a defining characteristic of the new ecclesiology even while many Anabaptists were still sword-bearers.

THE HISTORICAL DEVELOPMENT OF ANABAPTISM AS DEFENSELESS CHRISTIANITY

Although in different ways, and stimulated by differing impulses, Anabaptism in the major theaters emerged as a new ecclesial reality. Stated most simply, it was an ecclesial vision and practice that rejected the established church and with it the identification of the cause of Christianity with those structures and features of the contemporary social order, which they deemed to be disobedient to the rule of Christ. Instead, Anabaptist ecclesiology developed as a contrast community, which was shaped by spirit-empowered loyalty to the narrative of Jesus, and which came to exist as a communal structure that interacted with the established church and with the social order from a position of separation or difference.

It is necessary to emphasize here again that this sense of separation or difference from the established church and the social order is not intrinsically a stance of withdrawal but rather a stance of engagement or witness. The church cannot be a witness or pose an alternative unless it develops a self-understanding distinct from the perceived disobedience of the surrounding society as well as from those arenas of the church itself which have been assimilated to that disobedience.[14] We will return to this point later.

Swiss Anabaptism

Among the earliest reforming issues raised by the individuals who became Anabaptists in Zurich were objections to the payment of the tithe and the hiring of pastors.[15] The tithe—or church tax—collected by the head of the diocese in Zurich went to pay, among other things, the salaries of ministers. Some of the outlying parishes objected to paying the tithe, which was integrally related to the hiring of ministers. In moves toward autonomy, some of the outlying parishes claimed the right to hire their own pastors. They objected, in other words, to paying an involuntary tax that paid the salary of a pastor whom they had no voice in choosing. These issues concerned authority, and more than any other they led to the break between Ulrich Zwingli and the radicals who became Anabaptists.

Meanwhile, as is well known, within the city of Zurich, the Bible-reading circle that included Conrad Grebel, Felix Mantz, Andreas Castleberger, and others developed concerns about the sacraments of the mass and of infant baptism. Here their norm of appeal was the New Testament, with a particular focus on the words of Matthew 28:19. When applied literally, this text requires adult baptism—the command to make disciples clearly precedes the injunction to baptize these new disciples, and only adults could be taught to obey all the commandments.[16] Here the nascent Anabaptists' concern appears to be unqualified and actual obedience to the Scripture and to the words of Jesus.

Authority is also a factor. It was a question of authority when Zwingli advised that the city council would determine when and how reform of the Lord 's Supper was carried out, and when those who had withheld baptism of their children were commanded to have them baptized within eight days under penalty of the law. It was this authoritative edict from the authorities of Zurich that precipitated the "rebaptisms" of 21 January 1525, which marks the beginning of the Anabaptist reformation and the formal beginning of what in a few years would become a new and distinctive ecclesiology.

Other rebaptisms followed those of 21 January 1525. A short-lived Anabaptism came into being in Zollikon. Another, different Anabaptism took root in Waldshut, with distinctive, albeit mutually influential, communities of Anabaptist dissenters appearing in other areas as well. The Peasants' War challenged the prevailing institutions of the church and of the social order as peasants called for economic restructuring. Some survivors of the Peasants' War found Anabaptism attractive. At least one of the congregations—perhaps the one at Zol-likon—developed a congregational order that called for a common treasury.[17]

From these various efforts at reform—some successful, some failures, some explicitly within the church concerning the sacraments, others emerging from the forces of social reform that produced the Peasants' War—would appear a distinctive ecclesiology for those who became Anabaptists. The various emerging and mutually influential communities in their various locations moved at different speeds toward an Anabaptist ecclesiology without being pressed in this by some doctrinal office or other central ecclesiastical authority of their communal network. Some tried longer than others to produce reform by means of cooperation with civil authorities, but those who became Anabaptists eventually abandoned this approach. It is this ecclesiology, which sought to renew a church whose practices of faithfulness were not constrained either by civil authority or by privileged theological or ecclesiastical elites, that was consolidated and given explicit articulation in the Schleitheim *Brotherly Union* of 24 February 1527.

This ecclesiology was one in which the local congregation, and the broader network to which it belonged, claimed the authority and the ability to govern its own affairs, independent of both the civil authorities and of the church established and protected by such authorities. The first re-baptisms of 21 January 1525 may have been about bringing the practice of baptism into conformity with a New Testament pattern. But stressing voluntary adult baptism also implied an uncoerced and unprotected community of resource-sharing believers. Within a few short years, those who accepted rebaptism were choosing to enter and to build a church that chose its own leaders without regard for the authorities in Zurich and that practiced economic sharing as an alternative to a property-based security protected by the sword.[18] Baptism became the mode of entry to this church.

Anabaptists were harassed, exiled, or killed for "re-baptism," that is, for claiming to abandon the established church to enter a renewed, separated church. In effect, from the perspective of civil authorities, Anabaptists were threatening one of the institutions—the state-sponsored church—that gave order to society. Baptism was the means of establishing this new church, and baptism was a symbol of the right and capacity of the new church to control its own spiritual and economic affairs. While it was said that Anabaptists were killed for practicing re-baptism, what actually got them killed was defying the authorities that presumed to establish the church and defying the state church established by civil authorities for the whole of society.

The teaching and example of Jesus, along with other New Testament materials, became the primary norm of appeal for defining this new church that depended on neither civil nor established church authorities. By no means were all these Anabaptists *Stäbler* or staff-bearing pacifists. However, from the letter signed by Conrad Grebel, Felix Mantz, and five others to Thomas Müntzer in September 1524[19] to the Schleitheim *Brotherly Union* of February 1527, there developed a strand of Anabaptist teaching about defenselessness and rejection of the sword, based on appeal to the teaching of the New Testament and becoming elaborated with greater complexity and increasing consensus. Appealing in particular to the teaching and example of Jesus, as supported by a gently shepherded community of accountability and economic sharing, the commitment to defenselessness became a defining characteristic of Swiss Anabaptism, shaping both its concrete communal practices and its ongoing theological development.

South German and Moravian Anabaptism

A somewhat different route to nonviolent ecclesial Anabaptism appears in South Germany and Moravia. One impulse was heightened endtime speculation—the expectation of the near return of Jesus. That expectation occurred amid or was triggered by the religious and social unrest across southern Germany that has come to be called the Peasants' War. After the massacre of 6000 peasants at Frankenhausen on 15 May 1525, many of Hans Hut's followers came from the ranks of folks who still harbored the social goals of this movement or who were otherwise disillusioned with the established church that had supported those who suppressed the peasant revolt.

The clearest ecclesial Anabaptist manifestation developed in Moravia with those groups that eventually took the name of

Hutterites. Jacob Hutter's converts often came from areas impacted by the reform program of Michael Gaismair. Those joining Anabaptism in this context would be seeking a community that held the promise of the failed economic concerns from the peasant movement. Leaders such as Jacob Hutter reordered the desire for revolutionary economic justice along the lines of a voluntary community of goods unprotected by the sword of defense or governance, a vision that James Stayer has shown was not unrelated to the increasing emphasis on economic sharing among the Swiss Brethren.

As refugee colonies in Moravia, these Anabaptists soon became a model of a churchly community that claimed authority to control its own affairs, independent of both state authorities and the established church. Uncoerced adult baptism was the mode of entry to these religious communities. Their pursuit and persecution by civil authorities was due to their separation from and rejection of civil authority and rejection of the state church established by that authority. Rebaptism, the ritual of entry into the Anabaptist community, became the symbol of subordinate separation from established political and economic authority.

Dutch Anabaptism

Anabaptism in Münster was a socio-political, economic event, an effort to legislate Anabaptist convictions for all citizens, including the abolishment of private property and monogamous marriage, and to defend this posture with the sword. In turn, Anabaptist Münster's rejection of established ecclesial authority was suppressed militarily by the Prince-Bishop of Münster Franz von Waldeck.

These tragic events marked Menno Simons. Sparked by the sacramentarian movement which opposed visible church ceremonies, within two years of his ordination to the priesthood in 1524, Menno developed serious doubts about the Lord's Supper as taught in the established church. Then he began to doubt the practice of baptizing infants, spurred especially by the execution in 1531 of Sikke Freerkes Snijder for being rebaptized. But it was mass executions after an uprising related to Münster in early April 1535, where he saw people dying for false faith, that finally provoked Menno to act. Even so it was another nine months before he left the established (Catholic) church in January 1536 to join the fledgling Anabaptist movement.

This was a radical shift in ecclesial identity and self-understanding for Menno, we suggest. It was not sufficient merely to reform the sacraments from within the established church. Menno joined a movement in progress that held the promise of becoming a renewed *ekklesia* beholden neither to civil authorities or the established church and organized instead around penitent and regenerated obedience to Jesus Christ, a church "without spot of wrinkle." In joining and leading this movement, Menno was also reforming and reshaping the failed effort at legislated Anabaptism in Münster.

The persecution of the movement Menno joined was said to focus on rebaptism. But those baptisms signaled the rejection of the established church and the attendant challenge to civil authority that established that church.

None of these three Anabaptist movements—in Switzerland, Moravia, the Low Countries—developed unproblematically from an orderly and singular biblical vision. Those Anabaptist leaders who read and discussed the Bible did so in specific social contexts that differed in their structural reflection of disobedience to the gospel by religious and civil authorities on the one hand, and in popular resistance to those forms of disobedience on the other.

Nevertheless, for all of these geographically disparate and vulnerably related communities of faith, the struggle to make a visible witness to the reign of God they discovered in the biblical story of Jesus led them in the direction of defenseless separation from an integration of church and civil authority they viewed as corrupted and compromised. Amid a new-found interest in the Bible, assertions of local independence, failed social and economic reforms, the sacramentarian movement, and other dramatic events in the sixteenth-century historical landscape Anabaptist communities of all kinds came to adopt and to strengthen a conviction that the whole story of Jesus' life, death, and resurrection defines the church of Jesus Christ.

In these efforts at reform was a trial-and-error methodology of a seeking to discover what it meant to be empowered by the Holy Spirit to live out of the story of Jesus. In some cases, as with the Grebel circle, one could perhaps point to an urban, cosmopolitan reading of the New Testament that sought to reform the worship practices of the Zurich parish. In the case of South German Anabaptism, one can identify mystical appropriations of gospel convictions that refocused the commoners' aspirations for economic justice in terms that eventually would lead to Hutterite communes. In the Low Countries, Menno's restructuring of Melchiorite and Davidite Anabaptism[20] can be seen as a stabilizing biblical response to both highly subjective sacramentarianism and dangerously violent revolutionary Anabaptism.

In each case, a kind of culmination was reached in which there is an identifiable Anabaptist community in each of the three main theatres of Anabaptist activity. This community professed separation from the established church and refused to accept the intervention of civil authorities in its churchly affairs. Moreover this community had begun to produce texts which explained and justified its existence in biblical and even theological terms.

It is in the context of this trial-and-error methodology, this effort to understand what it meant to be the separated church shaped by the story of Jesus, that Hans Denck's often-cited statement about discipleship seems particularly apt. One comes to knowledge of God through a means, Denck said. "But the Means is Christ, whom none can truly know except he follow him with his life. And no one can follow him except insofar as one previously knows him."[21] This statement is not the anti-intellectual, anti-theological formula that it is sometimes made out to be. Rather, it reflects the way that human beings actually learn things.

A young couple embarks on marriage without knowing really what it will entail—they learn by doing how to deal with changes and growth in a spouse that were totally unforeseen when they set out to learn about marriage. High school students arrive at the university, committed to acquiring a university education, but they have little understanding of the work it will entail and the changes they will have to make. Young people see the televised celebrity of athletes and actors and musicians and decide to follow such careers—but without any idea of the hard work and perseverance required, most drop out when they learn what it is about. People need an idea where they are going—or they could not begin the process. But what the process really entails they learn only in the doing.

The individuals who became Anabaptists committed themselves in a variety of controversial ways to live out of the story of Jesus Christ. It was not always clear what such a commitment would mean, and they did not all understand this commitment in the same way. But impelled by forces of various kinds, some religious, others social and economic, Anabaptists of many different stripes started seeking what it meant to live by the power of God and the Holy Spirit out of that particular story, typically by accepting baptism by confession of faith, despite the record of their own encounter as infants with water in church.

The product was several versions of the separated, visible church. This church professed its independence of civil and established church authorities and implemented in a variety of ways the economic sharing, rejection of violence, and love of enemies that they found in the New Testament, particularly in the story of Jesus Christ. This visible church was understood to be the manifestation in the world of the reign of God that Jesus had announced and enacted in his life.

Although each of us has written elsewhere about many of these details, and although we believe that understanding this complex path of development is useful, our paradigm focuses more on this product than on the details of the path traveled to attain it. The paradigm we advocate is not based on nor does it claim to have found an early manifestation as a defined essence that is then actualized. Rather, our paradigm describes the product, which results from multiple paths of development. The product emerged for the Anabaptists more as an effort to discover who they were as disciples of Jesus in their particular circumstances than as an effort to implement a full-blown, founding vision.

The claim that the teaching and example of Jesus constituted the model for the spirit-empowered conduct of those who professed the name of Jesus pulled the issue of the sword into the heart of the discussion about the character of Anabaptism and of the Christian life as defined by Anabaptists. Perhaps the earliest manifestations of rejection of the sword may have appeared in the letter to Thomas Müntzer, in which Conrad Grebel, Felix Mantz, and their colleagues declare that followers of Jesus are not to defend themselves with the sword.

This impulse is found many other places as well—in the Schleitheim articles, in writings of Michael Sattler and later Pilgram Marpeck. Take Marpeck in his "Confession" of 1532:

> I conclude before my God that worldly power, for all its work, is not needed in the kingdom of Christ whose kingdom is not of this world, and I further conclude that all who attempt to preserve the kingdom of Christ by stooping to the governing authority will be punished for it and come to shame. For our citizenship is in heaven.[22]

The impulse appeared in a very different way in the celestial flesh Christology of Menno Simons, which we discuss in more detail in what follows. The full title of *Martyrs Mirror* refers to "defenseless Christians called Anabaptists." This strand of thought came to be an identifying characteristic of Anabaptism. Anabaptists refused to bear the sword and engage in warfare, even when called to do so on behalf of a Christian magistrate in defense of their homeland or city.

At the same time, some—even many—early Anabaptists. including Balthasar Hubmaier and the Anabaptists of Münster, never espoused following the teachings and example of Jesus with respect to exercise of the sword. James Stayer's important work, *Anabaptists and the Sword*,[23] lays out a number of positions of Anabaptist sword-bearers. Such examples may appear to undercut Anabaptism as a pacifist movement. Our paradigm does not claim that nonviolence was accepted by all individuals identified as Anabaptist. But neither does our paradigm allow the plural panoply of multiple Anabaptisms of polygenesis to relativize the nonviolence of Anabaptism. Rather, we are describing Anabaptism—whether violent or nonviolent—from the perspective of those Anabaptist communities that came to be committed to nonviolence, such as the Mennonites, Amish, Hutterites, and Brethren.

THE ECCLESIAL DEVELOPMENT OF
ANABAPTISM AS DEFENSELESS CHRISTIANITY

The term *ecclesial* from the name of our paradigm emphasizes the social-political dimension of Anabaptist ecclesiology.
It is more than an extension of any of several versions of medieval piety, more than a culmination of the magisterial reformation. It is not reducible to a theological core shared with all
Christians, nor is it merely the common denominator of historical observation or a distillation of what happened in the sixteenth century. We believe that Anabaptism was in fact a church
of Jesus Christ that posed a distinctive and visible enactment of
defenseless faithfulness to the way of Jesus. The German word
Gemeinde encompasses what we mean by "ecclesial" Anabaptism—emphasizing the communal gathering of members of
Christ's body for the purposes of God. Ultimately, we believe
that describing Anabaptism as a church—a *Gemeinde* or an
ekklesia—is most faithful to the sixteenth-century sources themselves. Here we offer a brief survey of a variety of images and
metaphors by which Anabaptists in the three primary geographical theaters shaped their ecclesial self-understanding.

The Swiss Brethren developed an understanding of the
church as a separated and defenseless "little flock" of brothers
and sisters organized by their uncoerced unity in Christ and led
by "shepherds" chosen by and accountable to the congregation.
When seven of these radicals wrote to Thomas Müntzer in 1524,
it was stressed that "the gospel and its adherents should not be
protected by the sword" and that instead "true believing Christians are sheep among wolves, sheep for the slaughter."[24]

The Schleitheim *Brotherly Union* of 1527 elaborated this rejection of violence through conscientious objection to the magistrate's sword and by routinizing the speedy local selection of
ministers in response to authorities' efforts to destroy the community's leadership: "But if the shepherd should be driven
away or led to the Lord by the cross, at the same hour another
shall be ordained to his place, so that the little flock and the little flock of God may not be destroyed, but be preserved by
warning and be consoled."[25]

Furthermore, nothing more forceful than the ban was to be
used to protect the faithful unity of the church: "Within the per-

fection of Christ only the ban is used for the admonition and exclusion of the one who has sinned, without the death of the
flesh, simply the warning and the command to sin no more."[26]
In the congregational order that eventually circulated with the
Schleitheim *Brotherly Union*, some of the concrete implications
of this approach to church life were worked out: frequent gatherings for discussion of the Scriptures and mutual exhortation,
support for good conduct through loving admonition, sharing
of all capital and assets in common, and sharing a simple meal
and the Lord's Supper during assembly. All of these practices
enabled an increasing identification with the gathering of believers into a visible vulnerable collective of shared wealth,
wisdom, meals, and spiritual support that posed a contrast
with the surrounding civic/religious order.

Among the Hutterite communities in Moravia, this contrast community was most fully organized as an alternative
economic order, rooted in the willing subjection of believers to
one another in a fellowship grounded in the shared life of the
Trinity:

> Just so, the Father has nothing for himself, but everything
> he has, he has with the Son. Likewise, the Son has nothing
> for himself, but all he has, he has with the Father and with
> all who have fellowship with him. All who have fellow-
> ship with him, and with each other, have likewise nothing
> for themselves, but they have all things with their Master
> and with those who have fellowship with them.[27]

For Riedemann, this renewed and reordered community of
goods—the church—is a "lamp, a star of light, and a lantern of
righteousness in which the light of grace is held up to the whole
world" and through which "the light of Christ" is "shed abroad
to others."[28]

The Dutch Anabaptist tradition offered visions of the
church that confirmed and at times contrasted with the visions
that had emerged among the Swiss Brethren and the Hutterites.
Anna Janz in a testament to her son before she was executed
pleaded with him to join "a poor, simple, cast-off little flock,
which is despised and rejected by the world," for "where you
hear of the cross, there is Christ."[29] Anna's injunction is echoed
and elaborated in the letter of Joriaen Simons to his son Simon:

"Look for the little flock, whose entire rule of life agrees with God's commandments, and whose ordinance or sacrament is in conformity with the command of Christ and the practice of the apostles; this is the true church of Christ, without spot or wrinkle."[30]

For Menno Simons, this assumption that the true church can only be faithful in the form of a "little flock" is confirmed by the fact that in "Scripture you will find that the number of the elect was always small and the number of the unrighteous very great."[31] Furthermore there are pastoral reasons that dictate the necessity of smallness for the truly regenerated congregation: "for where is the Christian pastor who does not know his sheep? And where is the Christian brother who does not know his Christian brother?"[32]

Menno grants the possibility that a pastor may not be able to know every single person, but he argues that "still, one brother should know the other" so that they can "observe, teach, admonish, comfort, and reprove each other, and seek each other's salvation; for this is the Word and unction of God."[33] Elsewhere Menno lists the signs of the true church as including pure doctrine, the scriptural use of sacramental signs, obedience to the Word, brotherly love, bold Christian confession, and persecution for the sake of the Word of God.[34]

But perhaps the most eloquent and original statement by Menno about the identity of the church is his account of the church as essentially a community of peace, since its ruler is the Prince of Peace:

> The Prince of Peace is Jesus Christ; His kingdom is the kingdom of peace, which is His church; His messengers are the messengers of peace; His Word is the word of peace; His body is the body of peace; His children are the seed of peace; and His inheritance and reward are the inheritance and reward of peace. In short, with this King, and in His kingdom and reign, it is nothing but peace. Everything that is seen, heard, and done is peace.[35]

The central feature of the church's mission, in other words, is following the Prince of Peace in every aspect of life together. This holistic vision of peace is an active vision, not a passive or negative one. In the same text where he advances his vision of a peace church, Menno elaborates on the practices of "those who are the Lord's church and body." These practices include serving the neighbor "not only with money and goods, but also after the example of their Lord and Head, Jesus Christ, in an evangelical manner, with life and blood."

Then comes the list of deeds of mercy that famously appears more than once in Menno's writings: "They entertain those in distress. They take the stranger into their houses. They comfort the afflicted; help the needy; clothe the naked; feed the hungry; do not turn their face from the poor; do not despise their own flesh."[36] The church, in other words, is a generous and active community of gracious stewardship and social advocacy. Menno notes that even though much of the property of his community has been taken away by the authorities, still none that have joined the community "have been forced to beg."

This concern for the material and concrete well-being of everyone in the community as well as their neighbors is not a peripheral or a secondary matter for the church's identity, according to Menno: "If this is not Christian practice, then we may well abandon the whole Gospel of our Lord Jesus Christ, His holy sacraments, and the Christian name, and say that the precious merciful life of all saints is a fantasy and dream. Oh no. God is love; and he that dwelleth in love dwelleth in God and God in him."[37]

The nonviolent community of stewardship described by Menno again and again is called by Dirk Philips "the congregation of God"—(de Ghemeynte Godts)—which "has come together from all people," and was "first begun by God in heaven with the angels." This congregation is a "congregation of saints, namely, the angels in heaven and believing born-again people on earth who are renewed according to the image of God" and who are "joined together through Jesus Christ."[38]

For Dirk, this congregation by definition exists in a state of antagonism with the forces aligned against God, since for him there are only two kinds of congregations: "God's people and the devil's people."[39] For Dirk, God's people are necessarily persecuted by the devil's people, since there is eternal enmity between the children of Eve (the church) and the snake (the devil): "conversely, God's children conquer the snake and its seed, the world and all that is in it, through the blood of the lamb."[40]

The struggle against and ultimate victory of God's people over the works of the devil is made visible in the daily life and practices of the church, for Dirk. His treatise on the congregation of God includes seven ordnances: the teaching of God's Word by ministers ordained by the local congregation, the use of sacraments such as baptism and the Lord's Supper, the washing of one another's feet, evangelical separation from those who reject the church, love for brothers and sisters expressed through both spiritual and economic support, the keeping of all of Jesus' commandments, and the expectation of suffering.[41]

Dirk elaborates on the expectation of suffering by explaining the righteous must suffer precisely because by definition they refuse to protect themselves through violence or domination over others. He observes that "no congregation of the Lord may have domination over the consciences of people with an external sword, nor compel the unbeliever to faith with violence, nor kill the false prophets with the sword and fire."[42] Instead the believing community is an eschatological community of love and unity: "For the congregation is first of all the Holy City, whose citizens are the believers in Christ, and the household companions of God, and will therefore be called a city, because like a city it must be united; the citizens must be firmly attached to each other."[43] The people of this city are from a city to come and are thus "at peace to dwell with Abraham, Isaac, and Jacob in tabernacles and to be strangers upon the earth. For they seek another city which has one foundation, whose builder and creator is God."[44]

While there are differences of inflection among these various Anabaptist visions of the church, it is possible to recognize some recurring themes. The emerging form of church among Anabaptists in all of the major theaters of Anabaptist origins was a vulnerable and nonviolent community of spiritually and economically attached Christian believers. They posed a visible and disconcerting alternative to the corrupted alliance between church and political authority that had for centuries coercively identified all people in a given region with Christendom. From

Conrad Grebel and Felix Mantz to Menno Simons there is a vision for a church with the political and spiritual courage to distinguish itself from the exploitative and violent social arrangements that had been masquerading as Christian and to thus reengage the church in a costly struggle against the "world," a struggle that was energized by the triumph of Jesus Christ over the forces of sin and death and by the power of the Holy Spirit.

The new ecclesiology of Anabaptism quite clearly shaped the practices of the church. But this ecclesiology also had an impact on Anabaptist theology itself, that is, on the ways that Anabaptists thought about and expressed the meaning of Jesus Christ and what it meant to be his disciples. We now turn to the emerging, distinct theology of Anabaptism, showing how their new ecclesiology reshaped the inherited tradition of classical orthodoxy. Anabaptist ecclesiology indeed revealed itself in new theological beginnings.

THE THEOLOGICAL NOVELTY OF ANABAPTISM AS DEFENSELESS CHRISTIANITY

It has been suggested that Anabaptists did not think theologically nor develop new theological directions but "simply" accepted and repeated the standard creeds and formulas of Christendom.[45] That suggestion is incorrect on two accounts. As this section will sketch briefly, Anabaptists did think theologically, and they did not merely repeat the standard formulas and creeds of Christendom.[46] It is true that Anabaptists did not write theology with a stated purpose of producing a new theology for a new ecclesiology. A significant body of evidence exists, however, showing that their theological writing contained new elements and revisions, which reflected the changed understanding of the church that had dawned on early Anabaptist leaders while they studied the Scriptures together.[47]

Analysis of atonement theology in the writings of Michael Sattler, Hans Denck, Balthasar Hubmaier, and Hans Hut reveals significant theological differences among these Anabaptists. However, a significant and recurrent conviction also appears, which marks them as Anabaptists. Although expressed in very different ways, all four of these Anabaptists believed that salvation through Christ would result in a transformed life of the believer, a result that is not an optional outcome but an intrinsic part of the definition of salvation. Thus it is possible to argue that one aspect of their disagreements and disputes is an embryonic beginning of an Anabaptist effort to articulate a new understanding of atonement theology.[48]

The tract "On the Satisfaction of Christ," in *The Legacy of Michael Sattler*, indicates an approach to justification by faith that exceeds both medieval and Reformation imagery. Although the tract uses some imagery of satisfaction atonement, it stresses that what Jesus did for sinners is not a mere substitution. The believer also suffers with Christ. The tract affirms Lutheran justification by faith but also, in line with Catholic thought, stresses that faith will result in good works. These works "are not the work of man, but of God and Christ (through whose power a man does such works) and do not happen because through them man achieves something as his own, but rather because God through them wishes to give to man something of His own." What the sinner then does is done with Christ. Christ has "done enough" for sins, yet continually he will "day by day again do enough in His members and for them, until the end of the world." Thus this tract acknowledges concerns of both Catholics and Reformation Protestants while going beyond both Catholic sacramentalism and Lutheran fears of works righteousness.[49]

Similarly Arnold Snyder points to the way that schoolteacher Valerius integrates an Anabaptist emphasis on a new life, what has been called discipleship, into an image of satisfaction atonement. In response to forgiveness of sin, "there must be a 'proving' of the already-accomplished redemption by means of concrete response and action."[50] In such revisions of atonement theology, one can observe the beginning of a new theological direction that is missed if emphasis falls on Anabaptist agreements with other traditions.

Neal Blough's analysis of the theology of Pilgram Marpeck in *Christ in Our Midst* produces comparable results. Marpeck certainly presumes the standard view of the two natures of Christ and referred to Father, Son, and Holy Spirit in ways that fit within standard trinitarian theology. However, his interpretation and application of those doctrines indicates a specifically Anabaptist rather than Catholic or Lutheran orientation. Marpeck is responding to the spiritualists whose focus on the inner dimension of salvation undercut the meaning of externals, whether ceremonies such as baptism and Lord's Supper or ethical conduct such as rejection of the sword. In response, Marpeck argues that since God had become human in the incarnation, God has necessarily linked divine revelation to the outer and material realms of the world. Spiritual reality is then known through the material, and the humanity of Christ is the source of humanity's knowledge of God.

Thus ceremonies, which include such actions as preaching and reading Scripture as well as water baptism and Lord's Supper, are outward manifestations of Christian faith and a continuation of the incarnation, the presence of Christ in the world. Specifically included in these ceremonies is following Jesus or discipleship, including love of enemy as well as of neighbor, as the Holy Spirit gives the believer the power to keep the commandments of Jesus. "Thus," Blough says, "the notions of the humanity of Christ, faith, the church, the Holy Spirit and ethics are all closely related in Marpeck's theology."[51]

In a later chapter, Blough deals more specifically with Marpeck's atonement theology.[52] He argues that Marpeck's theology reflects the stress on Jesus as both savior and example that is found in medieval, monastic theology and in Anselm's satisfaction atonement. Marpeck portrays the death of Jesus as satisfying the wrath of God from Anselmian atonement. However, he stresses resurrection as an integral element of Christ's saving work and understands the Spirit's transformation of the believer so that the Christian actually lives the teaching of Christ in the world in a material way. These are elements of actual victory over sin that align Marpeck with the atonement motif Christus Victor rather than Anselmian satisfaction atonement. Marpeck agrees with Martin Luther that justification is by faith rather than works, but he is closer to the medieval monastic tradition in understanding the cross as ethical model as well as work of salvation.

However, Marpeck believes that faith results in actual transformation of the believer by the Holy Spirit, so that salvation manifests itself materially in history as the believer lives the commandments of Christ, including rejection of the sword for all believers. Such belief distinguishes Marpeck from both Luther and from medieval theology.[53] Blough writes,

> It is rather Anabaptist nonviolence, based on the cross as an example, which distinguishes Marpeck's soteriology from other protestant positions. Christ the Saviour and Christ the example, bearing his cross until death, excludes the recourse to violence.[54]

Marpeck's extensions of the humanity of Christ into an argument for ceremonies and a rejection of the sword, and into revisions of atonement imagery in the direction of Christus Victor, indicate that Marpeck charted a new theological path.[55] That path and the uniqueness of Marpeck's Anabaptist theology are much less visible if one chooses to emphasize his use of classic trinitarian imagery, or the two natures of Jesus, or atonement images as these are found in medieval theology.

Since Menno Simons represents a coalescing Anabaptist tradition, his willingness to adapt the received theological formula is noteworthy. Menno adopted a Christology that does not conform to standard criteria for correctness, at least as judged by the definition of the council of Chalcedon, whose key phrase asserted the two natures of Christ: humanity and deity. Menno had a trinitarian outlook, and he took pains to affirm the humanity and deity of Jesus.

On the other hand, Menno's Christology was certainly nonorthodox. He followed the "celestial flesh" Christology of the Melchiorite Anabaptist movement. Briefly stated, Menno believed that Jesus' flesh was human flesh, but it was a human flesh that he had brought with him from heaven. Thus the heavenly Word became flesh *in* Mary but not *of* Mary; Mary nourished Jesus' flesh, but the flesh came not from Mary but from heaven. Menno used the analogy of a field which receives seed from a sower; while the field nourishes and grows the crop, the seeds come from outside and are not of the nature of the field.[56]

The concern behind celestial-flesh Christology was to explain how the human and therefore sinful Mary could give birth to a human but sinless Jesus.[57] However, if one applies the definition of Chalcedon in strict fashion—that Jesus had two natures—Menno's view is unacceptable. For Menno, Jesus Christ is undivided in his nature, "a single person, God's own first-born Son and only begotten Son," consisting of "holy and saving flesh."[58] Menno justified his Christology with reference to one kind of medieval misunderstanding about human reproduction, namely that at conception, the male implanted a complete human being into the womb of the female, where it grew until ready for birth. With that model in mind, Menno believed that Jesus must have begun from the Word, which entered Mary and became flesh.

Menno's intention was to define Christology in such a way as to ensure the sinlessness of Jesus while also preserving the unity of Jesus' person. For Menno, emphasis on the flesh of Jesus affirmed his humanity, while the heavenly origin of the Word both affirmed Jesus' deity and also preserved the unity of Jesus' person. Menno wanted to defend the sinlessness of Jesus because he believed that the church founded by Jesus was a pure one and an extension of Jesus' work on earth. This church would then be separate or distinct from the social order rather than the church of Christendom that supported the social order.

Menno also described the process of change and conversion in the life of the sinner so that he or she is transformed in an incomplete way into the flesh of Christ, a transformation which will find its fulfillment at the return of Jesus. Hence Menno's Christology is oriented by what can be called discipleship—the idea that the earthly life of Jesus constitutes an example, an authority, and empowerment for the life of Christian believers. If one comes to Menno with the idea that new understandings of ecclesiology and of discipleship will provoke other theological changes, then it is quite possible to see Menno's peculiar Christology as not just an idiosyncrasy or an unlearned departure from orthodoxy but as the beginning of an effort to articulate an Anabaptist theology.

Some of the hymns from Passau, written by imprisoned Philippite Anabaptist refugees from Moravia and which were latter incorporated into the *Ausbund*, also reveal the willingness of Anabaptists to revise received, supposed standard theological formulas. The first hymn by Hans Betz, which became number 81 in the *Ausbund*, is an exposition of the Apostles' Creed but also much more than a mere recitation of the creed. The lyricist felt free to take considerable theological liberties with the text. Instead of referring to the members of the Trinity as "persons," he wrote of the three "names" of the Trinity, and the overall emphasis was to stress the unity of the Godhead.

In treating the humanity and deity of Jesus, Betz's mystical theology does not follow standard christological dogma. He says, for example, that "the Godhead cannot divide itself, . . . Christ's coming into this age happened only according to his humanity which he received." Christ "flowed out from God in the light and clear, bright brilliance which he covered with his pure humanity," and "as a cloud goes over the sun, so that it cannot be seen, thus here in this age was the light covered with humanity;" and when Jesus finished his suffering on earth, "he went back to the Father into eternity. Understand! Only according to his humanity has he again received glory."[59]

Betz's statements come very close to, if not actually, deviating from standard trinitarian and Chalcedonian theology. In traditional interpretation, reducing the persons of the Trinity to names would appear counter to the standard belief that each person of the Trinity embodies fully all the characteristics of the Godhead. In the fourth or fifth century it could have been condemned as modalism. And that either humanity or deity would defer to or be subsumed under or covered over by the other runs counter to the standard Chalcedonian interpretation. The usual interpretation is that Jesus is fully human and divine; neither attribute is changed or subsumed under the other at any point from the beginning through earthly mission until ascension and return to unity with God.

However, Betz's hymn also says that Jesus "was visible according to his humanity so that he might teach us." And one who stands in the power of God has faith in God "who has created him now through Christ . . . begotten him again to be his son since he fell from God through sin and came into his wrath." In other words, by God through Christ, the sinner is recreated into a child of God, and through the Holy Spirit is "enrolled . . . in the Church."[60] Such comments put a clear Anabaptist-oriented discipleship caste on an outline of the Apostles' Creed. One could argue either that this hymn shows that Anabaptists were theologically deviant, or that they intended to be orthodox because the Apostles' Creed was used. However, we suggest a third interpretation, namely that the theological liberties taken in this hymn show that the experience of Anabaptism opened the door to new theological reflection, guided by commitment to faithful discipleship more than by theological correctness.

The second recorded Philipite hymn by Michael Schneider, which became number two in the *Ausbund*, dealt with the saving work of Christ and lends itself to similar observations. The hymn does feature the suffering of Jesus, in line with standard satisfaction atonement. However, this hymn accompanies that suffering with a strong discipleship motif. "Christ came to earth for this: to teach the right way, that one should leave one's sins and turn to him. . . . Whoever wants to have fellowship with him and be a partaker of his kingdom must also do like him here on this earth."[61]

Like in other Anabaptist theologizing we have observed, this suffering leads to a victory as the one who suffers with Christ experiences the triumph of the reign of God amid the tribulation of imprisonment. This victory through suffering goes beyond the received tradition of suffering with Christ and points in the theological direction of Christus Victor. These Philipite hymns in the *Ausbund* reveal a theology committed to a suffering resistance that both goes beyond the standard, received theology and the development of a resisting community that begins to express a new counter-establishment theology.

In line with these observations about Anabaptist theologizing, Gerald Mast's book, *Separation and the Sword in Anabaptist Persuasion*, presents a number of illustrations of how Anabaptists were developing a new theological tradition. The sketch here draws on the analysis of a major Hutterite statement, Peter Riedemann's *Account of Our Religion*. Riedemann belonged to the second generation of Hutterites, those who were consolidating an existing movement rather than participating in its creation. If Riedemann's writing shows theological development, that is a clear indication that the new Anabaptist ecclesiology had an impact on other theological issues.

Riedemann's confession was an exposition of the Apostles' Creed. By using this standard document, he no doubt meant the exposition to reassure the authorities of his and the Hutterites' orthodoxy. However, the *Account* is much more than a recitation of the creed. At virtually every turn, Riedeman makes additions and qualifications that take the creed in a Hutterite Anabaptist direction. This is clear in the way he turns a confession of God as Father into a statement of the necessity of living as an obedient child of God, or appeals to the relationship of Father and Son in the Trinity as the basis for community of goods and abandonment of private ownership of property.[62]

The significance of such revisions of the Apostles' Creed is missed if one assumes that Anabaptists are orthodox because they used a classic creed. In fact, Riedemann articulated the beginning of a new theological direction, a direction that becomes clear when one focuses on the revisions and additions, precisely on what is new in Riedemann's treatment of the Apostles' Creed. In fact, Anabaptists did not merely retain standard theological creeds and formulas with their new ecclesiology and a commitment to discipleship. Rather, as the many writings analyzed by Mast make clear, the new ecclesiology and a commitment to discipleship generated a distinctive theological direction.

In his introduction to *Martyrs Mirror*, Thielman J. van Braght began an introduction to his presentation of three Dutch Mennonite confessions—Flemish, Frisian, and Upper German—with a listing of the Apostles' Creed.[63] That presentation needs to be read in the context of the history of the Dutch confessional tradition. In this case, it appears more likely that the Mennonite confessions serve as a correction of what van Braght called "perverse interpretation" of the Creed by "erring persons going under the name of good Christians" rather than the presence of the Apostles' Creed being the assertion of a universal creedal authority.

By the time that van Braght's first edition of *Martyrs Mirror* appeared in 1660, Dutch Mennonites found themselves in some fifteen factions, divided by a range of issues of practice and theology. One way of understanding these factions is to see one cluster concerned more about the "living word" of Christian practice and another more concerned for correct doctrine of the "written word."[64] The factions had produced a long series of confessions of faith. Even as the divisions developed and continued, and there was a belief that the conflicted issues were important, Dutch Mennonites also had a sense that divisions were temporary. The confessions were written as attempts to bring factions together, as efforts to articulate a faith statement on which two or more sides could agree. The confessions van Braght included came from several sides and covered both sides of the debate between written word and living word.

Van Braght's introduction of the three confessions reads like an effort to conciliate between the confessional and anti-confessional positions. He inserts the Apostles' Creed in the context of competing impulses in Dutch Mennonitism. After an extensive discussion about the relationship between personal succession and doctrinal succession in the historical identity of the church, he states that any historically developed doctrine needs to be confirmed by the "true apostolic writings."[65] He then includes the Apostles' Creed, which he describes as the "ancient and simple creed" for which many Christians had "sacrificed their lives" but which had "in the course of time" been compromised by "perverse interpretations" and "erring persons going under the name of good Christians."[66]

But he does not cite the Apostles' Creed as the unquestioned given. On the contrary, the several Mennonite confessions are given as necessary corrections and elaborations on the Creed. "It has come that at this day there are found among those who are called Anabaptists, various confessions, which differ in style, but not in faith (we speak of the foundations of the same), in which confessions the creed set forth above is more fully interpreted and explained."[67] Perhaps his most precise statement of tactics is found in his introduction of the thirty-three-article confession from Peter Jansz Twisck, which emerged from heated debates between Twisck and Hans de Ries about the relationship between the convictions of martyrs and traditional Mennonite doctrine:

> Now to bring this account to an appropriate conclusion, we deem it not inadvisable to add here a certain Confession of Faith, which very probably, was once contained in

the History of the pious Anabaptist Martyrs, and is declared to have been the summary of their faith; though it may be (which we would not contradict), that they did not confess all said articles in precisely this form, but maintain more or less in regard to this or that point; which, however, if the true foundation of the same is retained, ought to, according to the nature of love, be borne with; especially in such persons who did not spare their dear lives, but gave them unto death, for their God and Saviour.[68]

That is, van Braght is aware of the passionate disagreements among the Dutch Anabaptists, which resulted in their many faith statements, and he reminds his readers that these Anabaptists were willing to die for these beliefs. However, van Braght's comment also means that creeds and confessions, including the Apostles' Creed, are not unquestioned and unchanging givens but undergo a continual process of updating and reflection on their meanings. Thus spousal shunning or celestial christological flesh, which seem unloving or peculiar and/or even scandalous today, are among highly particular commitments for some seventeenth-century Dutch Mennonites. Rather than showing deviation from practical or theological truths deemed universal or absolute, these contentious practices and doctrines should be recognized as efforts involved in the rethinking that results from the development of a new ecclesiology.

We need to remember that Dutch Anabaptist martyrs gave their lives not just for believers baptism and refusal to bear the sword, but also because they refused to accept that Jesus got his flesh from Mary. For these martyrs and for their descendants who accepted their view of the incarnation, the truth about God was inseparable from this conviction that Jesus' flesh came from heaven. This was not a negotiable or secondary matter. We may be tempted to distinguish essential from non-essential doctrines and to urge one another not to make a big deal about the minor issues. However, Thielman van Braght himself warns us against such a practice of defining the other side's doctrine as a nonessential when he acknowledges that the Mennonite opposition to excessive consumption and economic exploitation are regarded by "some worldly minded people" as "non-essential, unimportant for either good or evil, and therefore, allowable," a view he finds lamentable.[69]

Anabaptists did not have a specific *concept* of challenging the standard creeds and formulas and confessions of Christendom, and they did use and quote from the standard, received confessions such as the Apostles' Creed, the Nicene creed, or the Chalcedonian formula. However, the material cited here indicates that they did not simply repeat these formulations. They added to these formulas and confessions continually, which demonstrated the Anabaptists' sense of the inadequacy of the standard formulas and creeds.

It is also the case that they did not perceive the received formulas, creeds, and confessions as a standard "core" to which they were adding. Rather they typically considered that what they were adding was actually more important than the received formulations. That they considered the additions of more importance than the received formulations should be obvious—they held to these additions quite stubbornly despite great opposition, opposition that included martyrdom. As is said in the introduction to "the Five Articles of Faith" in the Hutterite *Chronicle,* "These five articles of faith are the reason for the great controversy between us and the world. All those of our church who have been executed by fire, water, or the sword were condemned because of these articles."[70] Anabaptists did not become martyrs because they held on to standard theological formulas. They became martyrs because they considered the standard theological formulas inadequate and developed statements that reflected their new understandings of ecclesiology and commitment to discipleship.

This discussion of theology is more than a recitation of what Anabaptists said about theology. It is also evidence that Anabaptists did indeed come to understand themselves as a separate church. Their sense of belonging to a new ecclesial movement enabled them—or perhaps freed them—to think creatively about theology, even if they did not proceed with the specific objective of posing an alternative theology to standard orthodoxy. Anabaptists did not have a concept of challenging the standard creeds and formulas. But the additions and revisions they made demonstrate that the new ecclesiology growing out of a commitment of discipleship to Jesus did provoke new thought.

This new thought in turn reveals the gaps and impulses they found lacking in the inherited formulas. It should be also clear from this account that Anabaptists expanded the truth of the gospel, rather than reduced it. They sought to preach and live the whole gospel, which was larger than what the creeds had managed to articulate.

It is possible, of course, to interpret Anabaptist theologizing differently. If one makes the assumption that theologizing about Jesus happens independent of ecclesiology and commitments to discipleship, then Anabaptist additions and revisions to the classic creeds and theological formulas will have a quite different meaning. To the extent that the classic creeds and formulas are visible within the additions and revisions, it can be argued that Anabaptists did not do distinct theologizing and merely repeated inherited theology. In this case, their revisions and additions to standard creeds and formulas take on an entirely different meaning. Any unique elements in Anabaptist theologizing are rendered unimportant, since of most importance is the stress on their agreement with standard formulas.

Further, their departures from standard formulas then become not evidence of independent and creative thinking on the basis of a new ecclesiology but rather evidence of their lack of theological sophistication and even evidence of deviant thinking. In the case of Menno, for example, rather than seeing him as attempting to chart a new direction, his theologizing becomes evidence that he was a poor theologian.[71]

However, we find the assumptions of this latter argument dubious. It seems a questionable argument to claim that Anabaptists would reject the received ecclesiology of Christendom while accepting in unquestioned fashion the creeds of the church they rejected. It is equally questionable that theologizing about the work of Christ would occur independent of impulses or concepts of ecclesiology and discipleship.

Our view is that theology is impacted by ecclesiology, that knowing Christ is shaped by following Christ, and that desire for faithful living should be the first and final motivation for theological argument. We believe that Anabaptist revisions of, deviations from, and additions to the inherited formulas indicate their creativity and independence of thought, as well as the formative influence of their new ecclesiology based on a commitment to live as disciples of Jesus Christ. That commitment leads again to discussion of the sword and sword bearers within a movement characterized by rejection of the sword.

THE NONVIOLENCE OF ECCLESIAL ANABAPTISM

Rejection of the sword was intrinsic to the life and teaching of Jesus. That discipleship to Jesus then means rejection of the sword for his followers was not in question for many early Anabaptists. What needs discussion is how rejection of the sword can constitute a distinct Anabaptist characteristic when many Anabaptists were in fact sword bearers. Recent popular treatments of Anabaptism have increasingly avoided making defenseless love an intrinsic or core commitment of Anabaptist communities—based on the view that "spirituality" should trump "ethics" in interpreting Anabaptism and that not all early Anabaptists, such as Balthasar Hubmaier, rejected the sword.[72]

One part of the answer to this tendency to downplay Anabaptist nonviolence is to highlight the prevailing Anabaptist conviction that the teaching and example of Jesus did serve as a norm for the church and the Christian life. It is that beginning assumption that makes the sword a contested issue in the first place. By the sixteenth century, the church of Christendom had made peace with the sword for more than a millennium. Of course the teachings of Jesus about loving enemies and not resisting evil with evil were kept alive in the prohibitions against fighting for the clergy and the religious. But these teachings were called "counsels," which the religious chose to obey but which were not considered binding on ordinary Christians.

Martin Luther wrote that for individual Christians themselves the teaching of Jesus applied, but that out of love for the neighbor, Christians were obligated to seize the sword to defend the neighbor. Christians had a duty to wield the sword of government to protect the righteous, to punish the wicked, and thus to preserve order in society. Writings in the Calvinist tradition went even further, making it a duty to rebel against and overthrow a tyrant. In the context of these arguments, that the sword was even a question among Anabaptists demonstrates the centrality of the whole teaching of Jesus in Anabaptist theologizing. In a sense, Anabaptists were the tradition whose identity came from conflict over this issue rather than mere acceptance of the received views on the sword.

Another part of the answer comes from insight gained from applying rhetorical analysis to issues of separation and the sword as discussed in Anabaptist argumentation. Mast's book, *Separation and the Sword in Anabaptist Persuasion,* shows how a variety of sometimes conflicting positions can exist within Anabaptism as different leaders and communities struggle to understand what it means to shape the church on the teaching and example of Jesus Christ.

Rhetorical analysis of the Schleitheim *Brotherly Union,* the first systematic statement of Anabaptist ecclesiology, identified two different stances toward the social order within the *Brotherly Union.*[73] In articles three and four, the church is perceived in a separation of *antagonism* to the surrounding disobedient social order. Church and world belong to two opposing systems, one of Christ and the other of Belial. These exist in opposition to each other, and a Christian must make a choice to belong to one or the other. In this mutually exclusive, antagonistic relationship, the church opposes the unfaithfulness of the rebellious social order, to which the sword belongs. That opposition is what it means to be Christian and to belong to the church of Jesus Christ.

Article six on the sword portrays another kind of separation, a separation of *complementarity* between church and world.[74] A complementary relationship is one in which two differently oriented and competing entities or groups are shown to fulfill differing functions and are thus not mutually exclusive. The Anabaptists at Schleitheim were pursuing a complementary relationship when they wrote that the sword was ordained of God for the preservation of order in society but was outside the perfection of Christ. In other words, Anabaptists were willing to acknowledge the authority of the civil government, including the authority to wield the sword, in exchange for legitimacy and recognition that they posed no threat to civil authority.[75]

Thus in working out the implications of a new ecclesiology Anabaptists used both antagonistic and complementary strategies in dealing with the social order. These two strategies were present already in the Schleitheim articles, and appear subsequently in Swiss, South German and Moravian, and Dutch Anabaptists, in documents of the Amish division, and in the later Mennonite confessional tradition into the eighteenth century.

This rhetorical analysis leads to three important points about peace and nonviolence for both sixteenth-century and contemporary Anabaptists. For one, this analysis shows how nonviolence is an intrinsic part of the Anabaptist story even when a number of Anabaptists were not pacifists. Rejection of the sword is not simply an item of debate to point out after one has listed the items all Anabaptists agreed on.[76] Because Anabaptists understood the church to be a visible embodiment of the whole gospel that contrasted with rebellious blindness of the surrounding society, discussion about the sword and violence could not but be intrinsic to Anabaptist self-understanding, even if Anabaptists differed with one another. Put differently, for most pacifist Anabaptists, the commitment to nonviolence was not somehow more optional or relative or secondary than other beliefs simply because some Anabaptists disagreed with the belief or articulated it differently.

Second, the rhetorical analysis that distinguishes the two forms of separation, that of antagonism and complementarity, also makes clear that separation does not necessarily mean withdrawal. Separation means first of all that the church identifies itself as distinct from the social order and, in the context of early modern Europe, distinct from the established church. That distinct church is not necessarily socially withdrawn, however. Both antagonism and complementariness, as forms of separation, concern ways the distinct church is involved in and interacting with the social order. A public statement of the social order as Belial is an engagement of witness that calls for conversion by magistrates who use the sword. The complementary response in article six, of acknowledging a role for the sword of civil authorities in exchange for tolerance, is also a posture of engagement with the social order.

Third, rhetorical analysis demonstrates that sixteenth-century Anabaptist positions on the sword—whether rejecting or accepting the sword—are not a trump card that definitively settles a contemporary debate. That is, the presence of one or the other of these views in the sixteenth century in and of itself does not prescribe that position for the contemporary church (just as discovering a statement in the Bible does not necessarily imply how Christians today should respond to the statement). Rather, just as when we read the Bible, Anabaptist texts challenge us to make choices about how we will express allegiance to the reign of God. No position from the sixteenth century can be absolutized for later emulation. Neither the complementary nor antagonistic stances in any of their variations were developed as static or unchanging answers. Each was a struggle for faithfulness of the church in a particular time and set of circumstances.

Understanding this characteristic of the stances in the sixteenth century should lay to rest any effort to determine the "correct" sixteenth-century answer for copying or recovery in the present. Seeking for the relevance of the Anabaptist story is not a matter of finding the correct stance and copying it but a matter of recognizing that we are always negotiating how the church exists or co-exists with the social order.

Finding relevance in the Anabaptist story is thus not a matter of identifying the right set of heroes to emulate or principles to adopt. It means rather to continue to live in an ongoing historical stream shaped by the same central posture of "following the Lamb wherever he goeth" that emerged from the Anabaptist story in the sixteenth century. This outlook is another expression of ongoing renewal and reform that comes from "looping back" to the narrative of Jesus.

CONCLUSION

Raising the issue of how to find relevance in the Anabaptist story means that we have come to the end of this chapter which focuses on defenseless Christianity in the history of the Radical Reformation. To recapitulate: We do not believe that Anabaptism can be reduced to an essence, or a series of essences, such as discipleship, communal ecclesiology, and nonresistance of Harold S. Bender's "Anabaptist Vision," nor C. Henry Smith's suggestion that Anabaptists represented the discovery of the freedom of the individual conscience.[77] Thus Anabaptism should not be defined by theology, by a common-denominator or theological core discovered through distilling the theology of all Anabaptists. Neither should Anabaptism be defined by making it the common denominator or the accumulation of all historical observation. Anabaptism is not best defined simply by describing what happened in the sixteenth century. Neither is the genius of Anabaptism deduced by identifying some medieval antecedent, such as monasticism or mysticism or spirituality, that has been lost from Anabaptism and now rediscovered and recovered for the twenty-first century.

Each of these suggestions, in differing ways, defines Anabaptism either in terms of some other movement or in terms of what already is. Each of these options limits Anabaptists to what is already given and thus limits the extent to which Anabaptism is a distinct movement defined by Spirit-guided newness. Each of these suggestions presents the future of Anabaptism in terms of the past. In such a context, the innovative appears—sometimes implicitly sometimes explicitly—as peripheral, questionable, or even heretical, instead of as a potential sign of the movement of the Holy Spirit.

In contrast, our paradigm treats Anabaptism as a distinct and Spirit-guided movement to follow Jesus Christ completely and visibly in the sixteenth century. While antecedents of various kinds are evident, we see Anabaptism as a new or renewed ecclesiology that emerged when early leaders who were studying the Bible together asked questions about social and ecclesial realities that led them to challenge the established church. The result was a dynamic Anabaptism, existing in multiple forms, but with change intending to be directed by practices understood to be empowered by and consistent with the life of Jesus. That Jesus' teaching and example applied to all Christians equally was a new element, which Anabaptists perhaps learned from the writings of Erasmus, but which they insisted on operationalizing, unlike Erasmus.[78]

In any case, it was an impulse that came to shape a new ecclesiology that rejected both the intervention of civil authorities in churchly affairs and the church established by those civil authorities. This church of Anabaptism, shaped by the teaching and example of Jesus as well as apostolic teaching in the New Testament, saw itself as a witness to the social order. Its foundation in the story of Jesus Christ made his teaching on love of enemies and rejection of the sword a formative issue for the church. This ecclesiology possessed the capacity to address all areas of life and thought. We have noted, for example, the church's capacity to address the economic concerns raised by peasants in the sixteenth century and the sense that this new ecclesiology required rethinking and revising and elaborating the traditional theological creeds and symbols.

Important to emphasize is that this Anabaptism is not a static movement that can be captured in a series of statements of essences. Of course we are describing it using propositional statements. But this Anabaptism is a dynamic movement. It existed in many forms in the sixteenth century. There is no normative version of it, although recent scholarship gives a measure of historical priority to Swiss Anabaptism. However, to be emphasized is that such historical priority does not signal priority of merit. A variety of forms existed, some in direct conflict with each other, which claimed to be the separated community of witness that is shaped by and living out of the life and body of Jesus Christ.

As such, the dynamic Anabaptism we have called nonviolent ecclesial Anabaptism and defenseless Christianity is not a single movement that can be copied or transported or restored or recovered. It is rather the beginning of a distinct historical tradition of witness to the social order and to the churches identified with the social order. This Anabaptism is a historical tradition that continues in the twenty-first century, in a number of forms around the world, sometimes as an independent church structure, other times as a visible motif within an established church structure. It is, in other words, a tradition that does not value tradition so much as attentiveness to the new creation that God is bringing about in contrast to the blind sinfulness of the present order.

Another element of the new ecclesiology concerned the role of women. True, the leaders were men and the major preserved writings were by men. Nonetheless, in the context of their age, women played unusually active roles in early Anabaptist communities. We can point, for example, to Ursula Jost in Strasbourg, whose forty-page book of prophetic visions inspired Melchior Hoffman. Another is Helena von Freyberg, a woman of noble birth from the Tirol. Helena hosted Anabaptist gatherings in her castle but willingly abandoned property and status as occasion demanded. While living in Augsburg, she hosted Anabaptist gatherings and served as a courier between Pilgram Marpeck and Caspar Schwenckfeld.

Many Anabaptist women died as martyrs. Fully one-third of Anabaptist martyrs mentioned in *Martyrs Mirror* are women, many of whom left behind published testimonies and letters, including Anna Janz who is quoted in this chapter. As early Anabaptism became consolidated into established communities, these more visible roles for women largely disappeared, with some notable exceptions and with a recovery of women's visibility and leadership in Mennonite and Brethren churches just beginning to occur in the twentieth century.[79]

We believe that this understanding of Anabaptism as found in the Radical Reformation still has much to say to the Mennonite church and to other Anabaptist churches in the twenty-first century that stand in the line of transmission from the sixteenth century. Perhaps most importantly, we believe that this paradigm speaks to the growing number of people who have become disillusioned with the traditions of the established churches and are finding meaning in the story of Anabaptism, the movement that originated as a witness to and a protest of the established churches. This continuation of Anabaptism in our own time is the subject of the next chapter.

NOTES

1. Social historians have expressed concerns that historical work done with a view to serving the church will fail to tell a complete story that includes embarrassing details and incidents. For example, in R. Emmet McLaughlin's lament for the passing of the current generation of prominent social historians, he states: "Without the intel-

lectual energy and academic respectability that social history provided, not to mention the close relationship to the Peasants' War that
reconnected Anabaptism with the larger society, there is a real danger that the field will become again an historical backwater in which
justifiable Mennonite concerns for identity and faith will overshadow the historians' commitment to understand the past, warts
and all." At this point we can assure readers that our discussion to
follow (as well as our other writings) does include the commonly recognized "warts" of Anabaptist history, such as the fact that many
early Anabaptists were not pacifists, the significant contribution of
the Peasants' War to the origin of Anabaptists, the emergence of Anabaptism via a trial-and-error rather than a programmatic beginning,
and of course the radical and violent events in the city of Münster.
For a discussion of these methodological issues, see the "Appendix:
On the So-Called Paradigmatic Void," at the end of the book.

2. Church history, and particularly Anabaptist history, is among
many applications of history to the present. We mention only two examples. The history curricula in United States schools present what
is called the American Revolutionary War of 1776 in such a way that
school children all learn that freedom depends on war, and without
war there will be no freedom. Similarly, the story of the terrorist acts
of September 11, 2001 is told in a way that justifies a "war on terror,"
invasions of Afghanistan and Iraq, domestic spying, huge spending
by the Pentagon, and much more. Each of these stories could be told
with much different emphases and applications.

3. Thieleman J. van Braght, *The Bloody Theater or Martyrs Mirror of
the Defenseless Christians Who Baptized Only Upon Confession of Faith,
and Who Suffered and Died for the Testimony of Jesus, Their Savior, from
the Time of Christ to the Year A.D. 1660*, trans. Joseph F. Sohm
(Scottdale, Pa.: Mennonite Publishing House, 1950) Along with the
title page, "Defenseless Christians" appears in the title of both parts
one and two, pp. 63, 663.

4. John H. Yoder, "Armaments and Eschatology," *Studies in Christian Ethics* 1 (1988): 58.

5. Robert Rhodes, "National Identity Focus of Resolution," *Mennonite Weekly Review*, 2007, 16 July 2007, 6.

6. Gerald Biesecker-Mast, *Separation and the Sword in Anabaptist
Persuasion: Radical Confessional Rhetoric from Schleitheim to Dordrecht*,
The C. Henry Smith Series, vol. 6 (Telford, Pa.: Cascadia Publishing
House, 2006); J. Denny Weaver, *Becoming Anabaptist: The Origin and
Significance of Sixteenth-Century Anabaptism*, 2nd ed., foreword by
William H. Willimon (Scottdale, Pa.: Herald Press, 2005); J. Denny
Weaver and Gerald Biesecker-Mast, eds., *Teaching Peace: Nonviolence
and the Liberal Arts* (Lanham, Md.: Rowman & Littlefield Publishers,

Inc., 2003).

7. Harold S. Bender, "The Anabaptist Vision," *Church History* 13, no. 1 (March 1944): 3-24; Harold S. Bender, "The Anabaptist Vision," *Mennonite Quarterly Review* 18, no. 2 (April 1944): 67-88. Reprinted as stand-alone pamphlet as Harold S. Bender, *The Anabaptist Vision* (Scottdale, Pa.: Herald Press, 1944) and as Harold S. Bender, "The Anabaptist Vision," in *The Recovery of the Anabaptist Vision: A Sixtieth Anniversary Tribute to Harold S. Bender*, ed. Guy F. Hershberger (Scottdale, Pa.: Herald Press, 1970), 29-54.

8. James M. Stayer, Werner O. Packull, and Klaus Deppermann, "From Monogenesis to Polygenesis: The Historical Discussion of Anabaptist Origins," *Mennonite Quarterly Review* 49, no. 2 (April 1975): 83-122.

9. We distinguish between strategies and tactics according to the work of Michel de Certeau who defined strategy as assuming a "place that can be circumscribed as proper and thus serve as the basis for generating relations with an exterior distinct from it (competitors, adversaries, "clientèles," "targets" or "objects" of research)." On the other hand, according to de Certeau, a tactic assumes a place that "belongs to the others" and thus "insinuates itself into the other's place, fragmentarily, without taking it over in its entirety, without being able to keep it at a distance." Michel de Certeau, *The Practice of Everyday Life* (Berkeley: University of California Press, 1984), xix. Put simply Anabaptist tactics were more like the improvised responses of the civil rights movement to the changing actions of racist authorities than like market- and survey-driven strategies of public relations firms seeking to sell a product or promote a political figure.

10. C. Arnold Snyder, *Anabaptist History and Theology: An Introduction* (Kitchener, Ont.: Pandora Press, 1995), 379-80.

11. Snyder, *Anabaptist History and Theology*, 402-4.

12. From a different rhetorical beginning point and with some different contemporary arguments in view, Ray Gingerich offers an Anabaptist vision for the twenty-first century with significant similarities and parallels to nonviolent ecclesial Anabaptism as defenseless Christianity. See Ray Gingerich, "The Canons of Anabaptism: Which Anabaptism? Whose Canon?" in *The Work of Jesus Christ in Anabaptist Perspective: Essays in Honor of J. Denny Weaver*, ed. Alain Epp Weaver and Gerald J. Mast (Telford, Pa.: Cascadia Publishing House; Scottdale, Pa.: Herald Press, 2008), 191-222.

13. Leland Harder, ed., *The Sources of Swiss Anabaptism: The Grebel Letters and Related Documents*, Classics of the Radical Reformation, vol. 4 (Scottdale, Pa.: Herald Press, 1985), 290.

14. For a more extensive discussion of this point, see Gerald Biesecker-Mast, "Critique and Subjection in Anabaptist Political Wit-

ness," in *Exiles in the Empire: Believers Church Perspectives on Politics*, ed. Nathan E. Yoder and Carol A. Scheppard, Studies in the Believers Church Tradition (Kitchener, Ont.: Pandora Press, 2006), 45-59.

15. This summary of historical developments in Zurich follows Weaver, *Becoming Anabaptist*, 33-45.

16. Abraham Friesen, *Erasmus, the Anabaptists, and the Great Commission* (Grand Rapids, Mich.: Wm. B. Eerdmans Pub. Co., 1988), 20-57

17. See Weaver, *Becoming Anabaptist*, 63-64; John H. Yoder, trans. and ed., *The Legacy of Michael Sattler*, Classics of the Radical Reformation, vol. 1 (Scottdale, Pa.: Herald Press, 1973), 44-45; Werner O. Packull, *Hutterite Beginnings: Communitarian Experiments During the Reformation* (Baltimore, Md.: The John Hopkins University Press, 1995), 33-46.

18. James Stayer has shown how economic sharing among many of the early Swiss Brethren more closely resembled the community of goods practiced eventually by the Hutterites than it did the mutual aid practiced by Dutch Mennonites. James M. Stayer, *The German Peasants' War and the Anabaptist Community of Goods*, McGill-Queen's Studies in the History of Religion, vol. 6 (Montreal & Kingston: McGill-Queen's University Press, 1991), 104.

19. Arnold Snyder has advanced the argument that Grebel was not a pacifist, and that the letter to Müntzer was a "mulligan stew" of items suggested by individuals whose signature applied only to their particular suggestions but did not signal agreement with the content of the letter as a whole. See C. Arnold Snyder, "The Birth and Evolution of Swiss Anabaptism, 1520–1530," *The Mennonite Quarterly Review* 80, no. 4 (October 2006): 526. Responses that raise questions concerning this argument include Gerald Biesecker-Mast, "Response to Snyder," *The Mennonite Quarterly Review* 80, no. 4 (October 2006): 651-54; Thomas Finger, "Response to Snyder," *The Mennonite Quarterly Review* 80, no. 4 (October 2006): 662-63; Ray Gingerich, "Response to Snyder," *The Mennonite Quarterly Review* 80, no. 4 (October 2006): 670-74; J. Denny Weaver, "Response to Snyder," *The Mennonite Quarterly Review* 80, no. 4 (October 2006): 685-90. While we dispute Snyder's assertion regarding Grebel, we can accept his conclusion that Felix Mantz was perhaps the most outspoken of the Zurich radicals on the point of biblical, cross-bearing pacifism.

20. For the story of Melchior Hoffmann and David Joris and their forms of Anabaptism, see Weaver, *Becoming Anabaptist*, 113-18, 134-41.

21. Hans Denck, *The Spiritual Legacy of Hans Denck: Interpretations and Translation of Key Texts*, interpreter and trans. Clarence Bauman, Studies in Medieval and Reformation Thought, vol. 47 (Leiden: E. J.

Brill, 1991), 113.

22. Pilgram Marpeck, *The Writings of Pilgram Marpeck*, ed. and trans. William Klassen and Walter Klaassen, Classics of the Reformation, vol. 2 (Scottdale, Pa.: Herald Press, 1978), 151.

23. James M. Stayer, *Anabaptists and the Sword* (Lawrence: Coronado Press, 1972).

24. Harder, *The Sources*, 290.

25. John H. Yoder, *The Legacy*, 39.

26. John H. Yoder, *The Legacy*, 39.

27. John J. Friesen, trans. and ed., *Peter Riedemann's Hutterite Confessions of Faith*, Classics of the Radical Reformation, vol. 9 (Scottdale, Pa.: Herald Press, 1999), 80.

28. Friesen, *Peter Riedemann*, 78.

29. van Braght, *Martyrs Mirror*, 454.

30. van Braght, *Martyrs Mirror*, 566.

31. Menno Simons, *The Complete Writings of Menno Simons c.1496–1561*, ed. John Christian Wenger, trans. Leonard Verduin, with biography by Harold S. Bender (Scottdale, Pa.: Herald Press, 1956), 732.

32. Menno Simons, *Complete Writings*, 732.

33. Menno Simons, *Complete Writings*, 732.

34. Menno Simons, *Complete Writings*, 743.

35. Menno Simons, *Complete Writings*, 554.

36. Menno Simons, *Complete Writings*, 558.

37. Menno Simons, *Complete Writings*, 559.

38. Cornelius J. Dyck, William E. Keeney, and Alvin Beachy, trans. and eds., *The Writings of Dirk Philips 1504–1568*, Classics of the Radical Reformation, vol. 6 (Scottdale, Pa.: Herald Press, 1992), 351-52.

39. Dyck, Keeney, and Beachy, *Writings of Dirk Philips*, 354.

40. Dyck, Keeney, and Beachy, *Writings of Dirk Philips*, 354.

41. Dyck, Keeney, and Beachy, *Writings of Dirk Philips*, 363-74.

42. Dyck, Keeney, and Beachy, *Writings of Dirk Philips*, 375.

43. Dyck, Keeney, and Beachy, *Writings of Dirk Philips*, 377.

44. Dyck, Keeney, and Beachy, *Writings of Dirk Philips*, 378.

45. "The Anabaptists did not feel called to the task of creative thinking in matters of doctrine. They were pleased simply to repeat the commonly accepted creeds." C. Arnold Snyder, *From Anabaptist Seed: The Historical Core of Anabaptist-Related Identity* (Kitchener, Ont.: Pandora Press, 1999), 49, see also 10; C. Arnold Snyder, "Beyond Polygenesis: Recovering the Unity and Diversity of Anabaptist Theology," in *Essays in Anabaptist Theology*, ed. H. Wayne Pipkin, Text Reader Series (Elkhart, Ind.: Institute of Mennonite Studies, 1994), 11.

46. Here in Chapter 2 and also in Chapter 3 we refer to "standard" formulations or "standard theology." The term "standard theology"

is a designation for all theological formulations that are presumed to be true as unquestioned givens, for theology that is presumed to be above any particular context and therefore accepted without having to be justified. Stated another way, standard theology is presumed to be general or universal, that is, applicable without qualification to all Christians everywhere. When accepted as true, its generalness or universality makes it "orthodox." Because of its great visibility both through expression in classic creeds and formulations and via articulation by "mainstream" theologians (such as Augustine, Anselm of Canterbury, Thomas Aquinas, Martin Luther, or John Calvin) who represent the churches of Christendom, what we are calling standard theology appears to rise above context and to be true simply because it comes from these "standard" spokesmen. In actuality, closer examination reveals that even the presumed general formulations of "standard theology" have a particular origin and historical context. In other words, the various and varied versions of what we are calling "standard" theology all have histories and particular contexts just as much as does the Anabaptist theology of defenseless Christianity.

47. This paragraph and portions of what follows were taken from or based on Weaver, *Becoming Anabaptist*, 208-17.

48. For analysis of Michael Sattler and Hans Denck in comparison with Martin Bucer, see J. Denny Weaver, "The Work of Christ: On the Difficulty of Identifying an Anabaptist Perspective," *Mennonite Quarterly Review* 59, no. 2 (April 1985): 107-29; for analysis of Balthasar Hubmaier and Hans Hut, see J. Denny Weaver, "Hubmaier Versus Hut on the Work of Christ: The Fifth Nicolsburg Article," *Archiv Für Reformationsgeschichte* 82 (1991): 171-92.

49. John H. Yoder, *The Legacy*, 108-18, quotes 113, 115.

50. C. Arnold Snyder, *Following in the Footsteps of Christ: The Anabaptist Tradition*, ed. Philip Sheldrake, Traditions of Christian Spirituality (Maryknoll, N.Y.: Orbis Books, 2004), 53-54, quote 54.

51. Neal Blough, *Christ in Our Midst: Incarnation, Church and Discipleship in the Theology of Pilgram Marpeck* (Kitchener, Ont.: Pandora Press, 2007), 33-46, quote 39. This book traces the sources and the development of Marpeck's emphasis on the humanity of Christ. An earlier version is Neal Blough, "Pilgram Marpeck, Martin Luther and the Humanity of Christ," *Mennonite Quarterly Review* 61, no. 2 (April 1987): 203-12.

52. See Blough, *Christ in Our Midst*, 92-223. See also Tom Finger, "Pilgram Marpeck and the Christus Victor Motif," *The Mennonite Quarterly Review* 78, no. 1 (January 2004): 53-78.

53. Blough cites medieval theologians including Anselm of Canterbury, Bernard of Clairvaux, and Thomas Aquinas to show that in

medieval theology the work of Christ as savior and as a ethical example are inseparable, a characteristic also present in Marpeck's thought. Marpeck's difference from medieval theology, Blough suggests, is that he considered the teaching of Jesus applicable to all Christians rather than being specifically applicable only to a limited class of Christians, namely clergy and monastics. See Blough, *Christ in Our Midst*, 206-21, esp. 206-9.

We suggest that additional aspects are involved. It appears that the medieval use of Jesus' ethical example stressed imitation of virtues such as charity or patience or humility rather than the particularity of his rejection of the sword as did Marpeck. Stress on such virtues opens the possibility of following the virtue while exercising the sword, as in using the sword out of love for the neighbor in an attitude of love and humility toward the enemy. In any case, it poses an interesting juxtaposition to quote Bernard of Clairvaux on the Sermon on the Mount as "Christ's teaching par excellence" in light of Bernard's vigorous preaching of the second Crusade, or to contrast Anselm's assertion of the importance of the example of Jesus' patient endurance of suffering with Anselm's attendance at war as a spectator sport in the company of Pope Urban II, who proclaimed the first Crusade. On Anselm as war spectator, see Anthony W. Bartlett, *Cross Purposes: The Violent Grammar of Christian Atonement* (Harrisburg, Pa.: Trinity Press International, 2001), 95-96.

54. Blough, *Christ in Our Midst*, 219.

55. Blough himself evaluates the evidence differently than the argument here. Blough acknowledges that Marpeck's extension of the humanity of Christ to include rejection of the sword clearly identifies Marpeck as an Anabaptist. But rather than suggesting that Marpeck or Anabaptists charted the beginning of a new theological movement, Blough chooses to stress the importance of classic theology and to stress how Anabaptists can or should be part of the "universal church." In particular, see the final chapter of Blough, *Christ in Our Midst*.

56. For Menno's writing on Christology, see Menno Simons, *Complete Writings*, 422-40, 487-98, 763-72, 792-834. For an analysis of Menno's Christology, see William Keeney, "The Incarnation, a Central Theological Concept," in *A Legacy of Faith: The Heritage of Menno Simons: Sixtieth Anniversary Tribute to Cornelius Krahn*, ed. Cornelius J. Dyck, Mennonite Historical Series, vol. 8 (Newton, Kan.: Faith and Life Press, 1962), 55-68. The argument for Menno given here first appeared in J. Denny Weaver, *Anabaptist Theology in Face of Postmodernity: A Proposal for the Third Millennium*, foreword by Glen Stassen, The C. Henry Smith Series, vol. 2 (Telford, Pa.: Pandora Press U.S., copublished Herald Press, 2000), 104-5. Mast expands significantly

and validates the argument in Gerald J. Mast, "Jesus' Flesh and the Faithful Church in the Theological Rhetoric of Menno Simons," in *The Work of Jesus Christ in Anabaptist Perspective: Essays in Honor of J. Denny Weaver*, ed. Alain Epp Weaver and Gerald J. Mast (Telford, Pa.: Cascadia Publishing House; Scottdale, Pa.: Herald Press, 2008), 173-90.

57. Traditional Catholic thought solved this problem in a different way. To give Jesus a sinless mother from whom he could then inherit sinless flesh, Catholic thought eventually posited the "immaculate conception" of Mary, in which the Holy Spirit miraculously interceded to prevent the transmission of original sin when Anne and Joachim, Mary's parents according to tradition, conceived her through sexual intercourse. The resultant sinless Mary could then give birth to a sinless son of her flesh.

58. Menno Simons, *Complete Writings*, 793, 820. For a more extensive discussion of Menno's celestial flesh Christology and how it relates to Anabaptist ecclesiology, see Mast, "Jesus' Flesh."

59. 1. Robert A. Riall, trans., Galen A. Peters, ed., *The Earliest Hymns of the* Ausbund: *Some Beautiful Christian Songs Composed and Sung in the Prison at Passau, Published in 1564*, Anabaptist Texts in Translation (Kitchener, Ont.: Pandora Press, 2003), 31, 48-49, 51, 53.

60. Riall and Peters, *Earliest Hymns*, 50, 53, 54.

61. Riall and Peters, *Earliest Hymns*, 62.

62. Biesecker-Mast, *Separation and the Sword*, 142-44, 145-46.

63. van Braght, *Martyrs Mirror*, 27.

64. Keith L. Sprunger, "Printing 'Not So Necessary': Dutch Anabaptists and the Telling of Martyr Stories," *The Mennonite Quarterly Review* 80, no. 2 (April 2006): 170.

65. van Braght, *Martyrs Mirror*, 26-27.

66. van Braght, *Martyrs Mirror*, 27.

67. van Braght, *Martyrs Mirror*, 27.

68. van Braght, *Martyrs Mirror*, 372.

69. van Braght, *Martyrs Mirror*, 10.

70. *The Chronicle of the Hutterian Brethren, Vol. 1*, ed. and trans. Hutterian Brethren (Rifton, N.Y.: Plough Publishing House, 1987), 251.

71. Thomas Finger is the latest in a long line of Mennonite scholars to regard celestial flesh Christology as embarrassing. Thomas Finger, "Confessions of Faith in the Anabaptist/Mennonite Tradition," *The Mennonite Quarterly Review* 76, no. 3 (July 2002): 283.

72. See for example, C. Arnold Snyder, "Signposts of Faith," *Leader* 6, no. 1 (Fall 2008): 2-4. Certainly it must be acknowledged that Snyder does mention loving enemies as a mark of Anabaptist discipleship. At the same time, he insists that spirituality is a prior and more significant focus of proper Anabaptist discipleship. The editor

of the magazine in which this article appears remarks on the absence of peace as a significant marker of Anabaptism for Snyder, although the editor seems to favor Snyder's decision to privilege "conversion" as a prior, more significant commitment than a commitment to peace. We see a defenseless Christian vision as not setting up a choice between privileging conversion or privileging peace. Conversion *per se* is as meaningless as the category of "spirituality," which could refer to the piety of Buddhists, Muslims, atheists, or Hare Krishnas. Spiritual conversion is certainly a commitment that Anabaptists share with practically all human beings from Osama bin Laden to George Bush who have changed or intensified their spiritual loyalties at some point in their life. But we do not think that emphasizing Anabaptist spirituality makes much more sense than emphasizing that Anabaptists believed things. Belief, conversion, and spiritual identity as such are not meaningful characterizations of a human community since practically every human community includes these dimensions of consciousness. We are convinced that the conversion experience of early Anabaptists was a specific conversion to the gospel of peace.

73. The following summary of arguments from *Separation and the Sword* is taken from J. Denny Weaver, *Becoming Anabaptist: The Origin and Significance of Sixteenth-Century Anabaptism* (Scottdale, Pa.: Herald Press, 1987), 200-203.

74. In Mast's book, *Separation and the Sword*, the term *dualism* is used to name mutually dependent and complementary relationships, thereby confusing ethicists who are used to thinking of dualism as a "good versus evil" view of the world.

75. Biesecker-Mast, *Separation and the Sword*, 101-8.

76. Rejection of the sword does not appear as a defining issue of Anabaptism when Arnold Snyder defines Anabaptist theology in terms of a core of shared beliefs. See Snyder, "Beyond Polygenesis," 12-16, and Snyder, *Anabaptist History and Theology*, 83-98.

77. C. Henry Smith, *Mennonites in History* (Scottdale, Pa.: Mennonite Book and Tract Society, 1907), 17-18.

78. Friesen, *Erasums, The Anbaptists, and the Great Commission*, 28.

79. On women in Anabaptism, see C. Arnold Snyder and Linda A. Huebert Hecht, eds., *Profiles of Anabaptist Women: Sixteenth-Century Reforming Pioneers*, Studies in Woman and Religion/Études sur les femmes et la religion, vol. 3 (Waterloo, Ont.: Published for the Canadian Corporation for Studies in Religion by Wilfrid Laurier University Press, 1996.)

Defenseless Christianity for Today's Peace Churches

"WHERE THERE IS NO VISION THE PEOPLE PERISH" (Prov. 29.18 KJV). Defenseless Christianity—that is, nonviolent redemptive practices motivated by and disciplined by the historically visible body of Jesus Christ (the faithful church)—is a paradigm that we have used to characterize sixteenth-century Anabaptism in its peaceful and biblical form. It is also a vision that we believe can inspire radical faithfulness among the contemporary peace churches, Mennonite Church USA, the Church of the Brethren, the Brethren in Christ, and other Anabaptist denominations or informal clusters of individuals and parachurch organizations in other denominations who are moved by the Anabaptist vision. Indeed, as a vision based on the life and story of Jesus Christ, we invite every believer who confesses the name of Jesus Christ to consider the life and perspective-changing good news we have characterized as defenseless Christianity.

Chapter 2 posed this paradigm as a way for the contemporary church to understand the sixteenth-century movements that gave birth to the modern peace churches. Equally important is providing a paradigm that assists the church today in extending the reconciling power of Jesus Christ to all who are alienated, angry, fearful, and lost.

Chapter 3 now turns to that task. The first section to follow sketches in broad outlines a vision of Christian defenselessness as a way for the contemporary church to live in the world. Subsequent sections then apply or extend this paradigm into several areas of significance for contemporary peace churches and nonviolent Christians everywhere. We believe that this perspective has the potential to impact all areas of life and thought of today's churches.

Given this broad horizon, we make no claim to comprehensiveness in what follows. The areas touched upon have current relevance, but readers are invited to extend our analysis to other areas and issues. Some sections of our discussion intersect with others and separate aspects of the same issue may appear in different sections. That arrangement of ideas reflects the complexity of the contemporary world and the lived messiness of faithful defenselessness, a feature of inhabiting what has been historically a minority position sometimes missed by frameworks that reduce Anabaptism to a handful of distinct viewpoints or an orthodox core.

ANABAPTISM AS DEFENSELESS CHRISTIANITY

That sixteenth-century Anabaptists rejected the state church and offered a visible alternative to the given social order are not particularly new elements in Anabaptist studies. What is new to our discussion here is placement of these particulars within the broader vision of noncoercive and reconciling love that was received by Anabaptists as a gift. Even Harold Bender's "Anabaptist Vision," with which we share so much in common, made nonresistance the third prong of the vision and was treated in a way that made it seem less significant than features of discipleship and a brotherhood-minded church.

We here do not reduce Anabaptism to any list of propositions or distilled essences, such as discipleship, community, or peace. Neither do we make it a specific inflection or application of prior orthodox spirituality. Rather we appropriate Anabaptism for today as a comprehensive reconciled and reconciling community of Christ followers that exists in multiple forms and articulates faith in a variety of ways. This communal form of Christian defenselessness is never finished but always in a process of becoming. That said, it is obviously still possible to describe characteristics and habits of this dynamic movement.

Anabaptism's rejection of the state church and of the idea that the social order is Christian, combined with the formation of a new and distinct society, mean that Anabaptism as defenseless Christianity is most obviously an ecclesiology—a theory and practice of the church. But the central practice that gives shape, substance, and meaning to this ecclesiology is the commitment (or profession of faith) to Jesus' life and teaching as the first and final source of truth. For Anabaptists, the will of God is revealed in the vulnerable humanity of Jesus, which forms the baseline by which Christians evaluate their own activities. Jesus, the one who came preaching peace, is the *norm of truth*, the image of the invisible God (Col. 1:15).

From following the account of Jesus' words in Matthew 28:19, where teaching precedes baptism, to accepting Jesus' teaching against the sword, Anabaptists from Manz and Sattler to Marpeck and Hutter to Menno and Dirk committed themselves to the truthfulness of the provocative and defenseless life of Jesus. This commitment and belief was given prime visibility in *The Anabaptist Vision*, when Harold S. Bender wrote that "fundamental" to the vision was the idea of "the essence of Christianity as discipleship."[1]

The idea of the normativeness and lordship of Jesus precisely in his defenseless servanthood undergirds John Howard Yoder's *Politics of Jesus*, and his description of the multiple ways that standard Christian ethics has claimed that the defenseless Jesus cannot be the norm for ethics.[2] Elsewhere, Yoder gave "follow[ing] the risen Jesus" as the basis for Anabaptist liberation from "Mars," "Mammon," "myself" and other self-protecting characteristics of the contemporary world.[3] This identification by and commitment to the story of Jesus who came to earth as a helpless child, challenged the overextended powers as a bold prophet, and refused the sword as a cross-bearing peacemaker is what makes Anabaptism fundamentally a

Christian tradition that addresses all people who claim the name of Jesus Christ.

It is this commitment to discipleship—to live out of and within the specific story of Jesus found in the Bible (and not some abstract theological figure that one simply accepts intellectually or emotionally)—that gives defenseless Christianity its particular identity as an ecclesiology, its particular generous and non-controlling way of being a church in the world. Many religious groups could be said to have an ecclesiology that is distinct. What gives specific shape and content to Anabaptist ecclesiology is its intent to live within and be shaped by the reconciling and serving practices of Jesus Christ. If most of the social order does not have this particular commitment to the nonviolent servant Jesus as an authoritative ethical and spiritual source, it follows almost as a matter of course that the church which accepts the Jesus found in the gospel accounts as that source will produce a new social reality. This reality will be a new community visibly different from the society in which it lives because this Jesus-following and Spirit-empowered community rejects violence of all kinds.

That is, to follow Jesus and to accept him as Lord involves a new way of life which expresses itself in redeemed attitudes and relationships among people both within and without the church. These attitudes and the practices they engender and nurture give the church its distinct character. This communal or social orientation does not deny individuality or the personal nature of one's faith, but it does mean that the individual's faith attains its fullness in terms of the *believing community* that practices the love and mutual service embodied by Jesus and empowered by his resurrection and the coming of the Holy Spirit.

Thus Harold Bender's second characteristic of the Anabaptist Vision was that "newness of life and applied Christianity" had created "a new concept of the church." John Howard Yoder expressed this concept of the church in terms of "liberation from the dominion of the mass." That is, the "Christian community is not Christendom. . . . It is the visible congregation of those who knowingly gather around the name, the teachings, and the memories of Jesus."[4] Baptism incorporates an individual into this serving and loving body of Christ.

This communal ecclesiology emerged in the sixteenth century as an alternative society both to the social order, with its government that exercised coercive and violent authority in religious affairs, and to the established church that depended on the sword of governance for support and pretended to encompass all of that society. But this Anabaptist ecclesiology is more than a rejection of the state church. This ecclesiology of the voluntary serving community of defenseless love also rejected the idea of a "Christian society," or a professed belief that the cause of the reign of God is identified with a particular nationality or ethnicity or political entity or social order or social class.

Stated differently, Anabaptism as defenseless Christianity does not depend on nor expect the structures of civil society to enforce its beliefs and practices, nor does it see the structures of the social order as the primary avenues through which to express and carry out its social concerns. Anabaptism as defenseless Christianity is a comprehensive society of a vulnerable and serving church that is visible because its distinct beliefs and practices are not dependent on structures of the social order but rather on the power of God as manifested in the victory of Jesus through cross and resurrection.

If the particular story of Jesus is a norm that gives the church its distinct character and shapes its communal practices, then peacemaking and the *rejection of violence* are incipient as the privileged manifestation of discipleship or of following the example of Jesus. This place for rejection of violence should be clear from our account above, which does not separate defenseless love from the core of Jesus' mission and life. Jesus' specific rejection of the violent option of the Zealots through his nonviolent confrontation of evil belongs in a central and necessary way to the peaceable nature of the reign of God revealed in Jesus' life and teaching. In the "Anabaptist Vision" Harold Bender expressed this idea as the "ethic of love and nonresistance . . . applied to all human relationships."[5] John Howard Yoder spoke of "liberation from the dominion of Mars."[6]

Since rejection of violence is intrinsic to the story and work of Jesus, we do not separate it from our confession of Jesus as Lord and norm. It may seem redundant to insist on explicitly attaching some version of nonviolence to our characterization of the One who has saved us. Surely it is obvious from reading the story of Jesus in the Bible that he loved his enemies and refused to take up the sword against them. Surely it is obvious from Paul's writings that it is precisely this dimension of Jesus' life that constitutes his triumph over the powers of sin and death and that we are then ourselves empowered as baptized disciples to follow against all of the expectations and demands of a violence-prone fallen world. But given the faith in violence of North American society, as well as Christian defense of national violence (including torture, see Greg Boyd in the Foreword), it is vital to state explicitly again and again that rejection of violence belongs intrinsically to the church living in the story of Jesus and empowered by the Spirit.

Central features of the Christ-following defenseless community include the enemy-loving servanthood of Jesus as ethical norm, the nonviolent and peacemaking church as a witness to the social order, and the inherently peaceful nature of the community of Jesus' followers. Additional convictions or principles inseparable from such a noncoercive and Christ-loving community are adult baptism, absence of hierarchy, Bible-based discernment, practicing discipline, freedom of conscience, and economic sharing. These features and characteristics constitute more than a list of propositions; they are not a creed or confession of faith to which Anabaptists give assent.

Living in a story shaped by these convictions is different from assenting to the principles as parts of a creed. These convictions function together to structure a distinct way of life, a way of living in the world that begins by accepting the Prince of Peace as Lord and the New Testament as the authoritative repository of writings on the life and teaching of Jesus. They describe an outlook that begins to collapse if any of any of these aspects are compromised.

These central convictions deal with relationships between people, so that the church truly is a new and loving humanity and is authenticated by the way it lives as much as by what it believes. To live in the Anabaptist story means to put oneself inside this ongoing narrative or drama and to embody its convictions—to stand where they stood or to put oneself in their social context—so that their lives of conformity to Christ shape the way the disciple today is conformed to Christ. As an analogy, consider the way a baseball player does much more than assent to the rules of the game and agree that they are true. To be a baseball player means to put oneself inside the rules both formal and informal, so that these rules shape the actions and activity of that baseball player. Even when players make errors and break the rules, it is still obvious that they are playing baseball and not ice hockey, although both sports employ sticks and hit round objects.

This depiction of a defenseless Anabaptist outlook does not describe a historical program to be imitated or transplanted. The Anabaptist tradition has a number of manifestations and expressions, as Chapter 2 explained. Each has significance as a particular manifestation of the nonviolent believers church. Yet, for several reasons, none of these historical expressions can be canonized as an absolutized or normative form. No composite or summary of common elements gleaned from multiple expressions constitutes a definitive description of Anabaptism. Neither can we identify a modern, normative form. Identifying a normative form carries several problems, some obvious, another more subtle. The only thing without which this church cannot exist is the presence and visibility of Christ's loving and peaceful humanity.

Identifying one form as normative would imply that we already knew that particular past forms and past answers also had the necessary capacity to respond to all new and future situations as well. But certainly past forms cannot contain answers for all future situations and contexts. Stated another way, presuming answers from a historical norm would reveal a great deal about the future—it would resemble the past. Further, forms that differed from the historical description would be intrinsically deviant rather than potentially new forms of faithful discipleship to Jesus Christ.

But there is another, more important and more profound reason for emphasizing that identifying an Anabaptist paradigm for the contemporary church does not mean imitating, transplanting, or recovering a normative historical version. Rather than being a fixed image, nonviolent ecclesial Anabaptism as defenseless Christianity is a stance toward the world. It is a way to live in the world—a posture—shaped by the peaceful story of Jesus Christ.

Such Anabaptism can and does have multiple expressions. But more significantly, it is always in the process of becoming, a process of determining how to live in the world. It is never a fixed entity that has determined definitively the form that the church should take. With the idea clearly in mind that this Anabaptist ecclesiology is shaped by the narrative of Jesus, it is an expression of Hans Denck's statement, cited in Chapter 2, of knowing Christ through discipleship. "But the Means is Christ, whom none can truly know except he follow him with his life. And no one can follow him except insofar as one previously knows him."[7] One knows that the church is to reflect Christ in the world, but what that means in practice becomes known only in actually living it out. The faithful church is always becoming Anabaptist, always becoming a defenseless witness to the Prince of Peace.

These reasons for rejecting the idea of a historically normative form may seem rather obvious. However, more subtly, in a move that is little recognized, a normative form appears that is not recognized as such. It emerges inevitably from the methodology that claims to be doing only neutral historical description of past events. This emergence of an unacknowledged historical norm occurs because the supposed neutral description inevitably becomes prescriptive and normative.

The shift happens apart from the author's intent and despite the author's claims of neutrality and absence of ideological intent. However, the supposed neutral description has assumed normative status as soon as or whenever one uses the description to say what Anabaptism is. Consider, for example, the emphasis on including all Anabaptists, including sword bearers, in some recent accounts of Anabaptist origins. Purportedly without an ideological bias, such presumed neutral accounts are claimed to be nonideological in contrast to Harold Bender's account of Anabaptism, in which Bender refused to consider sword-bearers such as Balthasar Hubmaier as true Anabaptists.[8]

However, when a presumed neutral, descriptive account correctly stresses that many early Anabaptists were participants in the Peasants' War and thus not pacifists, this account also verges on making normative statements about the character of Anabaptism. Among its points is that the character of early Anabaptism differed significantly from Bender's depiction of Anabaptism as a pacifist movement, a description that was the product of pacifist ideology.[9] The supposed neutral description of Anabaptism at this early moment in time has come to include interpretive statements about the character of Anabaptism—it was not a pacifist movement in its origins—and the descriptive is becoming interpretive and hence potentially normative apart from any intent of an author.[10]

The implication is that earlier accounts erred—Anabaptism was not the pacifist movement they depicted. This can establish support for modern arguments that the contemporary peace church should or can be less certain about its commitment to nonviolence and more willing to engage in the violent dimensions of national security. Those supposed neutral descriptions, and the application of these accounts to the modern context, may define a normative historical form. They risk, as it were, bringing it in unannounced through the back door.

The past of Anabaptism was not foreordained. Neither is the future as it would be if there were a normative form of Anabaptism, or if a historical description is presumed to define Anabaptism. Guiding the choices in becoming Anabaptist is the Anabaptist conviction about the peaceable servant Jesus' teaching and example as the authoritative source for the Christian life. In the decisions and choices that are made, there is a continual looping back to the narrative of Jesus, and asking again, in the new situation, how this narrative will shape our understanding and our actions in this new context.[11] This process of looping back is never finished. It is the process that should occur with every new situation. We are always in the process of thinking through again how to live out of the story of the Prince of Peace as it addresses the new situation in which we find ourselves.

If it appears that we are unable to discuss the meaning of the gospel of Jesus Christ without referring to the peace that Jesus Christ brings to the world, the impression is correct. We are convinced that in Anabaptism we discover the beginnings of a gospel witness that recovers the intrinsically defenseless and peacemaking qualities of the work of Jesus Christ that the church is called to make visible. The gospel of peace is not a gospel if it does not make peace. We are convinced that it is time for Anabaptists and fellow pilgrims to stop apologizing for this outrageously excessive good news and to proclaim the peace of Jesus Christ without compromise or qualification. "Peace on earth, goodwill to all people!" sang the angels in announcing the birth of Jesus. That is the message we believe all Christians are called to proclaim in words and in deeds as well.

SEPARATION FROM THE WORLD

The practice of a defenseless Christ-embodying church that is noncoercively distinct from the surrounding blinded world brings us to the idea of separation from the world. Anabaptism as defenseless Christianity is a separatist ecclesiology. However, the important point is that separation does not mean disengagement or withdrawal. Separation implies engagement with society. In fact, it is the sense of separation or being distinct that makes it possible for the church to engage with society. Without a sense of being separate or distinct, the church has no stance or posture from which to engage the world. If the church has no sense of being separate or distinct, the social order contains little or nothing toward which the church may direct its gifts of witness. As one of the most recognizably engaged of all Anabaptists, Pilgram Marpeck insisted, such engagement depends on separation: "This church is separated from the world, for it is a witness over it."[12]

Being "separate from the world" was the basis of defenseless sixteenth-century Anabaptist witness and challenge to social structures and the established church. Stated from the other side, for Anabaptists to be engaged with the society in which they live did not and does not mean necessarily joining society's structures, as in participating in office holding or exercising the sword of police work or of war. Engagement also occurs through challenge and maintaining a particular witness. In fact, for defenseless Anabaptists, engagement typically has meant refusing to accept the assumptions on which various kinds of political and religious institutions are based, specifically the assumption that violence is necessary to maintain social order.

While defenseless Anabaptism recognized that the use of violence can be said to serve those who are unwilling to live by the way of Christ, and even that God's providence is not suspended where the sword is exercised, defenseless Anabaptists refused to exercise even such "respectable" violence because it was outside "the perfection of Christ." The defenseless church is called to engage the world without relying on coercion or violence, to make the reconciling way of Jesus Christ visible without demanding that others accept it.

Mast's analysis reveals two kinds of separation or postures of engagement in Anabaptist history, namely those of antagonism and complementariness.[13] Both are present in numerous sixteenth-century writings. In a separation of *antagonism*, church and world belong to two different systems, one of Christ and the other of Belial, as Schleitheim said. These exist in opposition to each other, and a Christian must make a choice to belong to one or the other. In this mutually exclusive, antagonistic relationship, the church opposes the given and fallen social order, including specifically the authorities and powers that sustain it. That opposition is what it means to be Christian and to belong to the church of Jesus Christ.

On the other hand, a complementary relationship is one in which two differently oriented and competing entities or groups are shown to be distinctive but not mutually exclusive. The Anabaptists at Schleitheim were pursuing a complementary relationship with magistrates when they wrote that the sword was ordained by God for the preservation of order in society but was outside the perfection of Christ. In other words, in a complementary separation Anabaptists were willing to acknowledge the authority of the civil government, including the authority to wield the sword, in exchange for legitimacy and recognition that they posed no threat to civil authority.[14]

Context has much to say about which kind of separation needs to be stressed. In the society of socially tolerant United States, an antagonist posture may well be called for—opposing war and challenging the national faith in redemptive violence as well as challenging and posing alternatives to rampant consumerism, tax policies that favor the wealthy, social policies that underscore poverty and inadequate health care, and much more.

A host of examples come quickly to mind—individuals can join peace marches and antiwar protests. They can write letters to the editor and otherwise call attention to any number of issues such as racial profiling and police harassment of racial minorities. Some individuals withhold the percent of their tax money that goes to the military, or they advocate for the World Peace Tax Fund. High school students may choose not to participate in routine patriotic rituals such as the daily pledge of allegiance to the U.S. flag in school home rooms or may refuse to march with the band in the Memorial Day parade.

A congregation produces antiwar signs and makes them available through its website; or it supports a local Victim-Offender Reconciliation Program and also holds a not-in-our-name vigil in the town square every time the state executes a prisoner. On days when military recruiters visit the local high school, congregations can send counselors to talk about the alternatives of conscientious objection and voluntary service. The national denomination discusses health care for its pastors and members, issues position statements on peace issues, promotes publication of peace-oriented materials, supports the accompaniment work of Mennonite Central Committee and the anti-violence work of Christian Peacemaker Teams in Haiti,[15] Colombia, Mexico, the West Bank and elsewhere, and more.

In a society hostile to the church, where survival itself is at stake, the church might appropriately pursue a separation of complementarity. Some Christians in the now defunct communist Deutsche Democratische Republik [DDR], which officially prohibited Christianity, wanted to show that they were not a threat to the regime. Thus they engaged in respectful negotiations with the authorities and received permission to publish some biblical scholarship.[16] These same Christians opposed the smuggling of Bibles, an activity lauded on religious TV in the U.S., because it demonstrated to authorities in the DDR that Christians lied and were not trustworthy.

In a difficult setting such as war-torn Iraq or occupied West Bank, the nonviolent Christians of Christian Peacemaker

Teams might cooperate with a nonviolent Muslim team. In Iran, Christians can engage in respectful dialogue on theological issues with Muslim clerics. Actions of both antagonism and complementarity display Christians who respect the structures of others and who challenge the faith in violence of their own North American society.

In most cases there will no doubt be some combination of antagonistic and complementary approaches. At times, an irresolvable and fruitful tension might exist between the two stances. Whatever the case, a posture of separation from the given structures and powers that exercise authority and establish the "common sense" of the world as we know it, is a crucial liberating stance, a truth that sets us free to practice the whole gospel of reconciliation without compromise or apology.

Discipleship as Practice

In his book *Body Politics*, John Howard Yoder makes the claim that "the will of God for human socialness as a whole is prefigured by the shape to which the body of Christ is called" and that therefore "the people of God is called to be today what the world is called to be ultimately."[17] Yoder then offers as examples five practices of the church which make visible God's reign and whose approximations can be found in the best policies of the surrounding political order. The five practices, which Yoder acknowledges are not an exhaustive list, include binding and loosing, breaking bread, baptism, the fullness of Christ, and the rule of Paul.

We are convinced that this approach to the church's discipleship demonstrates most biblically and faithfully the proper relationship between the witnessing church and the surrounding disobedient society from which the church seeks to distinguish itself. In what follows, we restate Yoder's practices in ways that inflect the daily discipleship to which the life of the radical Anabaptist church calls its members. The ordering of practices follows the Anabaptist sequence learned from Matthew 28:19, namely that coming to adult faith and becoming a disciple of Jesus precedes baptism. These performance practices and the rules which accompany them are not discreet and in fact overlap considerably with one another.

Discovering the Truth

The truth, disciples are assured by Jesus, is what will make us free. Yet that truth cannot be discovered freely or individually. Christians discover or discern truth in the presence of two or three gathered together in the name of Christ around the Scriptures and under the moving of the Spirit. The skills associated with interpreting a text, listening to another's story, considering available policy options, fine-tuning a budget, debating opposing viewpoints, or questioning cultural or social trends—these are skills the church teaches its members and expects them to practice not only in Sunday school classes and small group or church committee meetings but also in workplaces, professional offices, classrooms, research labs, library stacks, archives, boardrooms, retail outlets, and factory floors.

Yoder has described the Pauline vision for such discernment and decision-making well: taking turns to listen to what each one has to say and then seeking a consensus agreement on the proper interpretation or the next steps.[18] This model Yoder acknowledges to have been developed perhaps most thoroughly by the Quakers, who have learned to apply this rule both to the discussions of their religious meetings and to the professional organizational contexts of Quaker-founded institutions such as colleges and relief organizations.

Of course this model of truth discovery does not always work smoothly or account adequately for the existence of disproportionate power or the stubbornness of the status quo. Yet it does provide a script for how defenseless Christians ought to perform the biblical expectation that the experiences and understandings of all people, even those bound by sin as we all have been, are gifts which contribute to the truthful discovery of a social body and thus to our own self-understanding.

While the skills and habits of the gathered discerning community are generalizable to a variety of public settings of decision-making or research analysis, the first and final epistemological community for Christians who seek to know the truth will be the church, that very particular body gathered around the biblical text, having invoked the presence of the Holy Spirit, and seeking to extend the plot of that biblical drama to the contemporary context.

There is no more significant preparation for the Christian life than teaching ourselves, our children, and newcomers the biblical story, studying and remembering this holy script, discussing and interpreting its message, and reliving its drama in singing, prayer, preaching, and other worshipful performances. For as we make life choices and participate in communities of work, the most significant motivation must derive from our self-understandings as sons and daughters of the God of Abraham, Isaac, and Jacob; and of Sarah, Ruth, and Rahab. The drama begun by Abraham when he followed the call of God to leave his home and travel to a better country, continued in the obedience and disobedience, the flourishing and exile, of God's people Israel. It was extended to all the nations in the life, death, and resurrection of Jesus Christ and in the life of Christ's body—the church—as the drama in which we are all called to take up our roles, wherever we happen to find ourselves living and working.

Respecting Life

Although in Anabaptist theology the practice of teaching and discovery must precede logically or chronologically the performance of baptism, the practice of baptism is nevertheless the basis and orienting point of every other practice of the church. For it is by submitting to the cleansing waters of baptism that we proclaim our allegiance to Christ, our identification with the people of God, and our renunciation of all violence and possessiveness on behalf of the new peaceable creation being born among and around us. It is by rising from our knees to the newness of life found in the resurrection that we anticipate a thousand replays of that dramatic moment in our own lives when we became members of Christ's crucified and risen body.

Again and again we will be called to submit to a cleansing tide offering us renewal and resurrection: a new creation. Yoder writes in *Body Politics* that "baptism is the formation of a new people whose newness and togetherness explicitly relativize prior stratification and classification."[19]

Furthermore, the new life made possible in baptism is experienced not only within the community of the church but is also a recognizable feature of the new creation that baptized eyes are capable of seeing all around us and in our contexts of work. Because we have been baptized, we will expect to discover and affirm forms of repentance, reconciliation, and social change in the world around us, a world being ordered by God.

At times our performance of being baptized will pose a nonviolent challenge to structures and authorities that enslave and harm. At other times being baptized will lead us to identify with public policies or organizational practices that more nearly acknowledge the divine image in everyone. A lawyer might develop his or her practice around cases that protect the lives of poor and disadvantaged people or do significant pro bono work for harassed undocumented immigrants.

We recall a member of our congregation in Bluffton, Ohio, who lost his job because he stood in solidarity with a friend who was experiencing discrimination. But we are also thinking of the manifold dramas—many of them full of both suffering and joy—associated with the Damascus Road anti-racism program being enacted year after year throughout Mennonite church institutions and specifically at Bluffton University, where we have been colleagues. These and other dramas of racial and social reconciliation derive strength when seen by Christians as reenactments of kneeling in submission to the cleansing waters of baptism and in anticipation of the new life to which we can then rise.

Likewise, the biblical call which Anabaptists have heard throughout their history to a defenseless life, to a renunciation of all self-protective violence, and to love for enemies should also be seen as a basic baptismal practice. As Jim S. Amstutz has so eloquently reminded us in his book *Threatened with Resurrection*, the impulse to self-preservation is in fact a denial of the reality of the resurrection, a reality we confess to be true in baptism and which we find ourselves to be threatened by, whenever our lives or interests are placed in danger by perceived enemies.[20]

The Anabaptist expectation that water baptism would be accompanied by a baptism of the spirit and followed ultimately by a baptism of blood, or what eighteenth-century Mennonite minister Henry Funk called a "baptism of the passion of Jesus," acknowledges exactly the link between baptism and defenseless cross-bearing love which we have been describing.[21] According to Funk, "under this baptism the Lord Jesus conquered and overcame the devil, and sin, and triumphed over them, and thereby opened a way into his everlasting kingdom, for the Fallen race of man; and in which way he commands them to follow him."[22] For Funk, "in this manner also is the affliction and suffering of the disciples and followers of Christ, which they endure for his sake, in bearing his cross after him, called a baptism."[23]

Baptism should thus be seen as the first and foundational vocational decision that any Christian makes. It is the dramatic moment of turning from Satan and worldly possessiveness to the resurrected Christ and the holy people of God that is reenacted in the life of the faithful church member again and again throughout the various arenas and stages of life.

Serving Others

The respect for the divine image in others that is made present through baptism shapes the servant stance taken by Jesus and enacted in the service of the Lord's Supper and in the ministry of sharing begun in the breaking of bread. Serving one another graciously at the Lord's Table and washing one another's feet with hospitality are churchly performances that anticipate similar performances of service in the surrounding world God is redeeming. The church potluck is a dramatic feast that Christians seek to enact more broadly in their struggle for economic justice and social equality. Relief work is the performance of labor as a gift that Christians seek to affirm whenever and wherever generosity of wealth and resources is to be found. The taking of an offering is a habit that will help believers in acting on behalf of fairer wealth redistribution amid capitalist acquisitiveness.

Christians who have learned the skills and habits of service to others through practicing such service within and on behalf of the body of Christ will discover many opportunities to perform service throughout their daily work. The term *servant leadership* along with the accompanying theory of leadership that has become prominent in management studies is an example of such a discovery that should be affirmed by Christians who seek to witness the in-breaking of God's reign wherever it appears. Anabaptist Pilgram Marpeck suggests that service includes our care for the whole creation, in that "the life and deeds of all true believers serve all creatures."[24]

We were inspired by the decision of a physician who lives in the Bluffton area to give up her medical practice in relatively comfortable and well-off Bluffton to set up a practice that serves people without medical insurance in the rust-belt city of Lima. Her decision is a witness to us all that the practices of baptism and breaking bread will lead both to small steps of service and to dramatic changes in lifestyle and occupation.

Others might follow that example by spending time serving with Habitat for Humanity or Mennonite Disaster Service rather than trying to get in as many overtime hours as possible for wages. Perhaps some family vacation time can teach service by engaging in a voluntary service project.

It is not the case that all work should be unpaid volunteering. But when we understand all of our work—whether paid or not—as service to God and neighbor, we will often develop different priorities than the consumption-focused, consumer-driven culture around us. Rather than focus our attention on actions that will increase status, income, and spending power, we will instead seek out opportunities for offering our gifts to all God's children and creatures.

Living in Community

Baptism makes possible a new humanity and a new community, shaped specifically by the posture of servanthood. At the same time it calls attention to the fact that as humans we have been "called and created for community."[25] There is in baptism a fundamental challenge to the myth of the singular individual heroically overcoming life's obstacles through wit and brawn or becoming self-actualized through a journey into the self. In baptism we celebrate the freedom and hope associated with life together, and we pledge ourselves to the humility and hospitality that characterize Christian community and which we receive as gifts from the Holy Spirit.

Perhaps the practice most associated with communal living in the church has been church discipline, including in the Anabaptist tradition the ban and shunning. And while we continue to think that some form of church discipline remains essential to a life of obedience to Christ, we are increasingly convinced that the most powerful forms of church discipline are those practices by which believers regularly gather and submit to each other in worship and praise of the Creator and Redeemer of life. Reciting the psalms or saying the Lord's Prayer together is a form of such discipline. Listening receptively to a sermon—even one the listener dislikes—is a form of such discipline. Learning to sing together with other members of a congregation is a form of such discipline—as is made clear by the many disagreements and church conflicts associated with musical style and habit.

David Ford has highlighted ways in which singing together is a form of Christian subjection to one another. Ford offers a reading of the well-known text from Ephesians 5 in which believers are to speak to one another "with Psalms, hymns and songs from the Spirit," making music from our hearts "to the Lord," while "giving thanks to God the Father at all times and for everything in the name of our Lord Jesus Christ."[26] Ford highlights the integration of mutual subjection, habit-forming repetition, gratitude, and bodily response that shapes the singing self. He writes: "Singing is a model of free obedience, of following with others along a way that rings true. In this the body often leads the self, and we find ourselves in a meaning which only gradually unfolds and pervades other spheres."[27]

Rowan Williams has pointed out that in singing psalms and hymns Christian congregations not only express the unity of our faith, despite ongoing division, but also establish our relationship to the communion of saints throughout history. By singing hymns and reciting Scripture together, believers give ourselves over to a language that we do not own, speech and rhythms from other times and places, and a memory of witness that transcends our own narrow perspective.[28] Thus singing and reading the Bible, as Williams writes, are spiritual disciplines "challenging the assumption that I—my conscious, willing ego—stand at the center of all patterns of meaning."[29]

Our experience of being decentered, of being not first of all singular individuals but members of the people of God, then becomes the basis for our actions and performances in many other contexts. We now understand ourselves to be acting as members of a people, and we will be able to encourage organizational committees as well as legislative bodies to act on behalf of the common good and the communities they represent, rather than on behalf of self-interest or personal advancement.

It follows that the first instinct of Christian believers when faced with life choices and professional decisions should not be to trust their initial impulse but rather to first consult with others. For Christians, the life of the believer is a team sport, a life always lived in reference to others and most of all in the context of belonging to the body of Christ. The Christian witness should thus be known in the marketplace as a witness of consultation, of checking on the views of others, of gathering people together, of bipartisanship, of seeking unity amid valued differences. The church nurtures such a public witness of mutual consultation by making a central feature of its own life the practice of discernment—in business meetings, in small groups, in ad hoc committees, or in what our congregation in Bluffton calls "discovery teams": groups of people gathered together to help a member in a significant life decision.

Becoming Priestly

The call to the freedom of communal truth-discovery, to life-affirming baptism, to life-embracing service, and to life-together in community, is one that in the biblical tradition comes as a call to sacrifice, to both receiving and giving away precisely the created life that is valued and celebrated. Thus, a defenseless Anabaptist church member accepts the invitation of Peter to join the royal priesthood of God's people, to offer our bodies as living sacrifices, and to make work and worship a singular offering of praise to God. "Render service with enthusiasm, as to the Lord," the writer of Ephesians admonishes, "knowing that whatever good we do, we will receive the same again from the Lord, whether we are slave or free" (6:7-8).

The priesthood to which we are all called needs pastors and shepherds, of course, those who have been called to "prepare

God's people for works of service, so that the body of Christ may be built up until we all reach unity in the faith and in the knowledge of the Son of God and become mature, attaining to the whole measure of the fullness of Christ" (Eph. 3.11-13). Still, the goal of the church is to make everyone a priest, and the pastoral ministry should be seen as a priestly task in the sense that pastors lead in preparing all believers for the priesthood.

THE PRACTICE OF NONVIOLENCE

Even though it should be clear by now that we understand nonviolence as intrinsic to a church that professes to live out of the narrative and life of Jesus Christ, it bears repeating that defenseless Christianity practices nonviolence in all of its actions. In fact, we argue that the nonviolence of the church is the characteristic of the church that qualifies all of its practices. This is simply another way of saying what the apostle Paul said so eloquently in his first letter to the Corinthians. No practice of faithfulness, not even the sacrifice of the body in martyrdom, is worth anything in the reign of God unless done in love (1 Cor. 13). The way of love and nonviolence encompasses a wide range of issues and practices. Some were mentioned above as examples of antagonistic and complementary separation. Here we provide a schematic description that includes issues not commonly mentioned as problems of violence.

In the book *Teaching Peace*, Glen Stassen and Michael Westmoreland-White developed a two-fold definition of violence. It is "(1) destruction to a victim and (2) by overpowering means. *Violence is destruction to a victim by means that overpower the victims' consent.*"[30] This definition includes the overt violence of war and the bodily harm done with weapons, but it also recognizes that systemic or structural injustices are also forms of violence. Although systemic violence is clearly distinguishable from the physical violence of lynching or war, it is important to acknowledge the real harm done to people by unjust structures and policies.

The theme of violence thus covers a wide range of issues. There is the direct violence that occurs with weapons, occurring at all levels from one individual harming another through weapons-wielding police forces to capital punishment and to massive violence among nations at an international level. Related and contributing to this violence on a national and international level are the major industries that design and manufacture war materials, for use not only by the United States but for sale to many other nations around the world. Direct violence may also include words that belittle and demean—whether an adult repeatedly declaring a child's worthlessness or the words commonly used to denigrate and belittle classes of people because of ethnicity, skin color, disability, or sexual orientation.

It is virtually self-evident that Anabaptism as defenseless Christianity opposes these forms of direct violence at all levels. That opposition can be passive—a refusal to participate. But in keeping with the engaged, activist character of discipleship that results in a lived witness to Jesus Christ in the world, in keeping with the separation of antagonism noted above, Anabaptism as defenseless Christianity can also engage in active opposition. That opposition includes the actions and activities mentioned earlier that demonstrate the separation of antagonism, which is another way to speak of practicing nonviolence. The opposition can include public demonstrations against war, a refusal to pay that portion of income taxes that supports the war effort, active work against spousal abuse, public manifestations against capital punishment, public school teachers who find creative ways to insert nonviolent views of history into the school curriculum, and much more.

Such opposition is limited only by the imagination of the disciples of Christ in defenseless Christianity. The life and witness of the community should then be living testimony to the futility of attempting to solve problems at any level with violence.

Large numbers of people encounter systemic and structural violence. Tax structures and social systems that favor the wealthy enforce the violence of poverty on those at the bottom of the social hierarchy. A specific example of this tax and budgetary violence is allocating many millions of dollars for sports stadiums with luxury boxes while claiming lack of funds for inner-city schools and services for poor people. Social practices of white privilege that silently hold back people of color and favor the white racial majority of the United States perpetrate the violence of racism. Social practices that favor men in the workplace perpetrate violence against women. The same applies to people who experience discrimination because of age or sexual orientation or disability. Both rhetoric and policies that blame "illegal aliens" for a host of domestic problems even as their labor is exploited by a number of industries enact violence against immigrants and citizens who look like immigrants. In terms of day-to-day living, people in North America may encounter such experiences of systemic violence more often than they do the direct violence of weapons.

Defenseless Christianity has the potential to confront these issues of domestic and systemic violence. As a community of faith that lives out of the life and story of Jesus, it is concerned for those without power—the widows and orphans and strangers of Jesus' time, who lacked political power in a world where political and economic status came through adult men. Today these people might include "illegal aliens," poor people, people without health insurance, persons with AIDS, victims of discrimination of various kinds, and more. The internal structures of defenseless Christian communities should reflect care for all members, regardless of social standing as defined by North American society. As a natural extension of this caring, the life of defenseless Christian communities should witness against and confront these kinds of structural and systemic violence.

This discussion of Anabaptism's confrontation of violence is only a bare outline of a wide range of issues. The point is not to address all dimensions of violence and response but rather to say that confrontation of and witness against the multiple dimensions of violence in North American society is an intrinsic dimension of the defenseless church of Jesus Christ as we understand it.

THEOLOGY FOR DEFENSELESS CHRISTIANITY

In our discussion of nonviolent Anabaptism in the sixteenth century, we pointed out that operating from within a new ecclesiology led Anabaptists to take theological initiatives. In fact such theological initiatives are one indication that Anabaptism as defenseless Christianity really is a new and distinctive ecclesiology rather than a variant of another movement. We believe that it is also true in the twenty-first century that this new ecclesiology has the capacity to shape theology—and that the theology emerging from Anabaptism as defenseless Christianity will reflect its visible ecclesiology and commitment to live out of the nonviolent life of Jesus.

Indications of a new theological direction for Anabaptism are not limited to the sixteenth century. In particular, Weaver's work has engaged that discussion at several points between the sixteenth-and twenty-first centuries. Eighteenth- and nineteenth-century Mennonite writing in North America presents examples like those observed in Chapter 2 from the sixteenth-century to the *Martyrs Mirror*. North American immigrant Henry Funk (d. 1760), who became a prosperous and prominent miller, landowner, and elder in the Franconia congregation, wrote his *Mirror of Baptism* (first published in German in 1744) at a time when the Mennonite outlook was in transition away from a sense that suffering constituted an intrinsic component of discipleship. As Mennonites developed relative wealth and were integrated into the larger Pennsylvania German society, leaders such as Funk developed the concept of "humility," borrowed in part from pietism, as an aspect of a life of nonresistant discipleship that confronted a society oriented by pride and ambition for worldly honor and wealth.

Earlier we quoted his writing to show a link between baptism and defenseless cross-bearing. Funk's writing certainly contained references to the standard satisfaction atonement, though reshaped to emphasize a life of nonresistant discipleship. But when he treated baptism in the passion of Christ, his language shifted to become much more like that of the classic Christus Victor (Christ victorious) emphasis. Thus he wrote that in his passion, "the Lord Jesus conquered and overcame the devil, sin, and triumphed over them, and thereby opened a way into his everlasting kingdom, for the fallen race of man; and in which way he commands them to follow him." Later he observed that

> The advantage of the cup of affliction, and baptism of
> blood, is worth more than it would be to gain the whole
> world. For by the baptism of the passion of Christ Jesus,
> and the shedding of his blood, when he died on the cross,
> he conquered the enemy, the devil, and redeemed
> mankind from the sin of Adam.[31]

A similar comment appears in Lancaster bishop Christian
Burkholder's (1746-1809) *Conversations on Saving Faith,* first
published in German in 1804. Burkholder's writing reflected
the pietist idiom adopted by Mennonites of his era. His language of sacrificial atonement appeared in the larger context of
a multifaceted view of regeneration of the sinner by Word,
Spirit, and Scripture, which must manifest itself in a changed
life. But in language resembling aspects of Christus Victor he
wrote that

> in the days of his incarnation, Christ set us the pattern of a
> lamb; and thus by endurance, suffering, and patient sub-
> mission, yea, by suffering the most painful and ignomin-
> ious death, on account of us sinners, he gained a tri-
> umphant victory over the world, sin, death, and the devil.

His following page admonished readers to follow the example
of Christ, love enemies, avoid all war and military service and
more.[32]

In *Keeping Salvation Ethical,* Weaver explored what eight
different Mennonite and Amish writers of the nineteenth century had to say about issues of violence and atonement theology.[33] The writers came from sixteenth-century Dutch-Russian
and Swiss Anabaptist lines of descent and included representa-
tives of both conservative and progressive streams of Amish
and Mennonites. Two observations were true about each of the
eight figures. Each had an understanding of atonement theology that could be placed within standard satisfaction atonement theology. However, in much the same way that a commitment to discipleship impelled Pilgram Marpeck or Peter Riedemann or Menno Simons and later Henry Funk and Christian
Burkholder to make additions and revisions to reflect discipleship and a rejection of the sword, the nineteenth-century Mennonite and Amish writers also made additions and revisions.

These distinguished their atonement theology from standard or common versions of satisfaction atonement.

These Mennonite revisions of inherited theology show that Anabaptists and Mennonites did think theologically and that they did much more than merely repeat the classic creeds and formulas. Their creative theological thinking begins, or at least opens the door to, the process of developing a new theology that reflects and emerges from the commitment to Jesus as norm of truth and an ecclesiology that embodies Jesus' teaching as a witness to the world.

For Weaver, stepping through that open door resulted in *The Nonviolent Atonement*.[34] This book stands in continuity with the longstanding Anabaptist efforts to revise standard (orthodox or classical) theology[35] so that it reflects a new ecclesiology and principles such as discipleship and nonviolence—but with an important difference. Rather than adding to or revising the prevailing, dominant atonement motif, *The Nonviolent Atonement* returns to the Bible to provide a new articulation of the work of Christ, with a view to making Jesus' rejection of the sword central and visible in articulation of his atoning work.

The new model makes in-depth use of the book of Revelation. The seven-headed dragon represents the Roman empire, the representative of the accumulated forces of evil in the world that are defeated by the resurrection of Jesus. A clear example of this victory appears in the dragon's defeat in heaven in Revelation 12:1-12, but the symbols actually refer to Rome, the church, and the victory of the resurrection of Jesus The Gospels tell this same story of Jesus from an earthly perspective. The life, death, and resurrection of Jesus reveal that his mission was to make visible the reign of God in the world. When the forces of evil headed by Rome sought to eliminate his existence by killing him, his resurrection became the triumph of the reign of God over the forces of evil including death. Believers are saved when they place themselves—and are placed by God—in this story and thus share in the victory of the reign of God in Christ's resurrection.

This model shares the victory motif of classic Christus Victor, but it is called narrative Christus Victor both to distinguish it from the classic image and also to stress that it begins with the narrative of Jesus. When salvation means to live in this narrative of Jesus, salvation has a material component in history, as discussed for Marpeck in Chapter 2, as well as an eschatological element as the believers share in the future culmination of the reign of God promised by his resurrection.

Narrative Christus Victor is a biblical and theological foundation for the understanding of the church in nonviolent ecclesial Anabaptism. Narrative Christus Victor describes the work of Christ in terms of his mission to make present the reign of God in the social order. Discipleship—living within the story of Jesus—then involves the disciple of Jesus in continuing that mission. And because the reign of God differs from the way institutions of the social order are operated, the church composed of the disciples of Jesus becomes a visible, separate entity in the world. In fact, its witness about the reign of God depends on that separation.

Stated another way, narrative Christus Victor, which lends itself to discipleship, has an understanding of being Christian, namely the life of discipleship, that actively engages the responsibility of the disciple of Jesus. Salvation comes from living within the story and resurrection of Jesus—and that means becoming actively engaged in the witness of Jesus to make visible God's rule in the world.

This engagement includes the examples of nonviolent witness mentioned throughout this book. It means that the church—understood to include all its components from the local congregation to the global church and all its multiple dimensions and entities—should comprehend itself as engaged in this life of witnessing to the presence of the peaceable reign of God in the world.

The atonement image of narrative Christus Victor, with its understanding of our salvation as participation in the work of Christ, stands in contrast to the understanding of salvation in any of the versions of satisfaction atonement theology derived from Anselm of Canterbury. In any of the multiple versions of satisfaction atonement, individuals escape eternal punishment and are thus "saved" when they accept the death of Jesus on their behalf as an offering of death or blood to God to satisfy God's offended honor or God's transgressed law.

In this image, then, the individual does little and accomplishes little and participates in little. Jesus is the only actor, and the sinner is passive while Jesus has acted. Salvation as defined by this atonement image implies little for the life of discipleship. The image of Jesus in this motif risks providing not much for the disciple beyond a harmful model of passive submission to suffering for victims of abuse and oppression.

Narrative Christus Victor as atonement motif features the image of an activist Jesus as a model for discipleship. The ministry of activist Jesus raised the status of women and Samaritans, who experienced discrimination (in different ways) in the society of his day. Activist Jesus poses a contrast to the Jesus of traditional satisfaction atonement, where his image models passive submission to injustice for victims of racial discrimination, spousal abuse, or military occupation.

Along with the emphasis on personal responsibility and engagement of the disciple of Jesus in narrative Christus Victor, which may sound to some hearers like righteousness by works or saving oneself, it is necessary to stress the importance of God's grace in the saving work of Christ. While the personal responsibility of the disciple of Jesus is engaged in the atonement motif called narrative Christus Victor, it is simultaneously evident that sinful human beings do not and cannot save themselves. We are utterly incapable of saving ourselves or of withstanding the rule of evil through our own power. If we are disciples of Jesus, if we are engaged in the witness of Jesus to make visible the reign of God in the world, it is because God in the person of the Holy Spirit has come and grabbed us and moved us onto God's side in the witness and struggle against evil.

This idea of human responsibility alongside of God's call in grace is an expression of what is sometimes called the paradox of grace. Paul the apostle expressed this paradox in 1 Corinthians 15:10: "But by the grace of God I am what I am, and his grace toward me has not been in vain. On the contrary, I worked harder than any of them—though it was not I, but the grace of God that is with me."

Narrative Christus Victor keeps fully in view the fact that discipleship to Jesus can lead to martyrdom. Its premise is based on the faithfulness of Jesus unto death in carrying out his mission. The disciple of Jesus does likewise. That commitment appears in a longer version of the title of *Martyrs Mirror, The Bloody Theater or Martyrs Mirror of the Defenseless Christians,* which also provides the designation of our paradigm of Anabaptism as defenseless Christianity.

The mention of the Holy Spirit here and elsewhere in these essays makes clear that narrative Christus Victor fits within the biblical imagery of the benediction in 2 Corinthians 13:13, which says, "The grace of the Lord Jesus Christ, the love of God, and the communion of the Holy Spirit be with all of you." This text and the baptismal formula of Matthew 28:9 constitute the important texts among the few in the New Testament that present God and Jesus Christ and the Spirit together in formulaic fashion. In later centuries theologians developed the language of Trinity and three Persons to explain the relationship of God and Jesus Christ and their Spirit. With the reference above to God's act through the Holy Spirit to move believers into discipleship to Jesus, narrative Christus Victor fits within this classic, three-fold language but remains somewhat closer to the biblical presentation.

This approach to an Anabaptist theology, which emphasizes the particular theological perspective that emerged from the new ecclesiology of Anabaptism, illustrates how the classic categories can be understood and reshaped with an Anabaptist theological perspective. It also further illustrates what was happening with the many additions to and revisions of classic theology by Anabaptists pointed out for the sixteenth century in Chapter 2 and for later centuries in this section of Chapter 3.[36]

The ecclesiology that develops from narrative Christus Victor is another way to see that the church of Anabaptism is distinct—separate—from the world but clearly engaged with the world. Ecclesiology emerging from narrative Christus Victor, building on the image of the church in the book of Revelation, makes most clear that it is the church and not a worldly entity such as a nation that is the means through which God works in the world.

Narrative Christus Victor and nonviolent ecclesial Anabaptism as defenseless Christianity underscore that for Anabaptism, there can be no concept of the "Christian nation." The gospel of Jesus Christ that gives birth to and is expressed in the church transcends and can in no way be limited to a political entity identified by national or geographical boundaries. Narrative Christus Victor as a theological expression of nonviolent ecclesial Anabaptism calls the disciples of Jesus to remember and confess that the highest loyalty is to Christ and not to the social order.

That the church of defenseless Christianity does not see a "Christian nation," that is, does not look to the state to enforce the church's social policies and practices, is evident in our approach to abortion. We agree with the pro-life movement that the number of abortions that take place in this country and the circumstances under which many abortions are performed are symptoms of a profound disregard for life in our society. We also believe that women alone should not be blamed—scapegoated—for this symptom of the problem of violence and disregard for life.

Thus those who oppose abortion should work for social policies and practices that reduce the perceived need for abortion, while the church can make sure to welcome children of all kinds and support parents of children in all circumstances of birth and rearing. We agree with the official position of Mennonite Church USA that asking the government to pass anti-abortion legislation is an instance of using coercion to force Christian convictions on others and is as counterproductive as trying to make the military illegal.

Seeing that narrative Christus Victor expresses a defenseless ecclesiology has given a theological foundation to the ecclesiology of Anabaptism as defenseless Christianity. But since narrative Christus Victor expresses an ecclesiology, it also means that one can talk about the ecclesiology of nonviolent ecclesial Anabaptism without going through the specific history of sixteenth-century Anabaptism. This point reflects John Howard Yoder's description of the relationship of a "radical reformation model" to a particular denominational identity:

> I therefore describe the radical reformation model as a paradigm of value for all ages and communions, rather than as an apology for a denomination claiming the last—or best—word. There is here no notion that all of the commu-

nities faithful to this vision relate genetically to one another, as a few of their teachers in the past argued.[37]

DEFENSELESS CHRISTIANITY
AND CONTEMPORARY STRUCTURES

We believe that the ecclesiology of nonviolent ecclesial Anabaptism implies several things for the way an Anabaptist denomination structures itself and the entities that comprise a contemporary denomination. For example, defenseless Christianity has implications for the structuring of Mennonite Church USA, the denomination to which both authors belong. We are aware that numerous Protestant denominations—especially those in the free church tradition—have struggled with the question of denominational structures in recent years. Our discussion of developments within one Mennonite denomination will, we trust, be helpful then not only to Mennonites but also to other Christian communities who seek faithful expressions of Christian love in their structures and institutions.

Borrowing a point from contemporary discussions of postmodernity, we would argue that every church organizational structure reflects particular values and assumptions. Stated negatively, no church organizational structure is simply neutral, equally suited for any structural purpose whether a business or a churchly denomination or a city government or a church-related university. The way an entity chooses to organize and govern itself says something about—and impacts the expressions of—the assumptions and values of that entity.

If methodological atheism is claimed for a particular governance model, such as the currently popular policy governance model developed by John Carver, from the perspective of Anabaptism as defenseless Christianity that claim of neutrality turns out to be problematic. This is because the Anabaptist concerns of discipleship-oriented and nonviolence-oriented ecclesiology are not integral dimensions of the model. The organization is then following a methodology developed by those for whom these issues are not relevant.

Mennonite history abounds with examples of the adoption of new structures representing new values that changed materially the way that the church understood itself. The adoption of a written constitution and the keeping of minutes changed the Mennonite identity of the movement led by John Ober-holtzer that left Franconia Conference and became a charter member of General Conference Mennonite Church. John Ruth has shown how such changes in polity strengthened an individualistic spiritual mindset and undermined Mennonite humility and nonresistance, even as they supported the emerging emphasis on mission and outreach.[38]

The church of the "parent" entities from which some components of the General Conference Mennonite Church split were themselves changed markedly through such factors as adoption of revivalist practices, entry into foreign and home mission work, the development of a denominational publication effort, and the adoption of a denominational structure and conference agencies with offices outside of local congregations.[39]

None of the changes in outlook were foreseen. Nonetheless, the philosophical-theological reorientation of the denomination was shaped by the new practices and new organizational structures. That is, although the new practices were not undertaken with a view to changing the philosophical-theological orientation of the denomination, inevitably the changes in church practices stimulated other changes. These changes can in fact be positive and for the better, even when they also have negative or problematic effects. The point is not to automatically resist such changes but to raise awareness so that leaders are aware of the potential for change and can attempt to guide the changes in ways that reflect the denomination's underlying commitments.

Following on the heels of the integration of Mennonite Church and General Conference Mennonite Church into Mennonite Church USA, the current time is again one that poses the potential for significant inadvertent or unintended reshaping of the values of the new denomination through the adoption of new structures of organization and governance. For several years, the denomination has been developing a national structure based on the methodology of John Carver to govern the way regional conferences relate to each other and to the national structure. The national office—and at least one Mennonite college—have adopted Carver's theory of administration. Known as policy governance, this approach stresses the practical authority of church leaders and agency directors with their staffs to run their organizations within broad constraints and goals established by the denomination or its various boards and committees.

This theory, informally called the "Carver method," starts with a board that appoints a chief executive officer and empowers that CEO to carry out the policy of the board. Advocates of this theory of governance laud its efficiency, its clear lines of authority, and the ability to assess whether the board's policies were implemented.

We believe, however, that the Carver theory has the potential to reorient the values of the denomination toward those of a business, emphasizing flexibility and agility in a competitive global marketplace instead of a community of believers seeking to be faithful and Spirit-guided stewards of the gospel in the context of a disobedient culture. To our way of thinking, Anabaptism as defenseless Christianity embraces the communal orientation of early Anabaptism, in which all major decisions were reached by an uncoerced group process. We are concerned that policy governance will distance the church's denominational leadership and agenda from the grassroots of the church and strengthen an increasing divide between the official denominational structures and the people in the pew that has characterized mainline Protestant denominations.

In fact, a controversial 2008 proposal that the Mennonite Church USA executive board abolish agency boards and place all of the church's agencies under the direct governance of the executive board, despite strong objections from the agencies themselves, illustrates the emergence of a business-oriented leadership culture in the denomination, focused on efficiency and marketing, rather than community and respect. To its credit, although the ultimate outcome is unknown as of this writing, the executive board postponed finalizing this decision following several days of consultation with members of agency boards. Such a capacity to take seriously the opinions and concerns of the whole body of Christ suggests that the Carver model has not completely destroyed the culture of respectful discussion and discernment that has assisted the church in building consensus in the past.

Whatever the outcome of current deliberations about church structure and polity, we agree with the conclusion of the research by a recent Bluffton graduate, Jason Moyer, that insofar as "Policy Governance is all about curtailing unpredictability on behalf of efficiency, then it is ill-suited to a church whose ultimate theological end is to be available to the workings of the Holy Spirit—the one who is, if it is anything, unpredictable."[40] We suggest that Mennonite Church USA funding challenges may be related to the loss of ownership and identification that many ordinary Mennonites feel toward a denomination that seems increasingly like a commercial enterprise in its image and language and modes of relationship.

If the leadership of the Mennonite church or of any denomination that seeks to follow the Prince of Peace wishes to consider what it would mean to be organized according to the life and teachings of Jesus Christ, those leaders should read the Pauline epistles once again, especially 1 Corinthians. Any improvisation on contemporary organizational models should be based on the priority of strengthening the capacity of the church to receive the gifts given by the Holy Spirit to each member of the body, even when those gifts seem to undermine such modern values as efficiency, consistency, and uniformity.

The ecclesial identity of defenseless Christianity is unapologetically the ecclesiology of a peace church. This peace church ecclesiology should be visible not only in the organizational practices of the church but also in the ways the church describes itself to its neighbors. Periodically, too often in fact, we hear of people who believe that too much emphasis on the denomination's peace stance is a hindrance to evangelism. That argument ought to be rejected out of hand. If the denomination is not a peace church, it is not reflecting the nonviolent story of Jesus as developed in defenseless Christianity. If evangelism is not about being a peace church, then the gospel proclaimed in that evangelism is not faithful to the life and story of Jesus.

The witness of a separate nonviolent ecclesiology implies the need for a concept of church discipline to strengthen the faithfulness of the church's witness. At the same time, the church must account for and honor minority voices. In the biblical story, the voice of the prophet, who was in the distinct minority, was frequently the one who best represented the will of Yahweh. In the sixteenth-century, Anabaptists, the spiritual progenitors of Mennonites and other peace churches, were a distinctly minority movement. The denominational structure must find a way to enable the minority and the majority to remain in dialogue within the church when each believes that it speaks the biblical word of Yahweh.

At this point, we refer specifically to the discussion of the acceptance of committed same-sex relationships within the denomination. While the majority opposes such relationships, there is a committed minority who clearly believe that it is their biblical and Christian calling to support such relationships. Rather than solving this problem by exclusion and denominational authority, we believe that Anabaptism as defenseless Christianity calls for the denomination not only to teach the official position of the church but also to listen to those who disagree with the position.

And while the essential defenselessness of the gospel of Jesus Christ cannot be rightly reconsidered in a church whose very identity is based in the cross-bearing and resurrected Christ, the practical meanings of defenselessness will surely be discussed and debated, including such vexing questions as the relationship of defenseless Christians to civil authority, the validity of police and military service for Christians, and the appropriate uses of the earth's limited resources.

For example, in the Mennonite church there are many who have dissented from the official position of the church and accepted positions in the military or police force. A defenseless church is not well-served by simply excommunicating such people, as was sometimes done in the past. Rather, the church should seek to engage these members in conversation, asking them to respond to the denomination's teaching position and then encouraging dialogue and discussion about these occupational choices. Especially should the church reach out to those who have experienced the physical and spiritual trauma of armed combat. The stories of those who have experienced war first-hand can help the church in the honesty and persuasiveness of its peace witness.

DEFENSELESS CHRISTIANITY AS WORLD VIEW

If nonviolent ecclesial Anabaptism as defenseless Christianity is a way to look at all of reality from the perspective of the nonviolent story of Jesus, then no professional occupation or academic discipline or mode of inquiry about the world falls outside the purview of this paradigm. If the defenseless Christian perspective truly impacts all of life, we should be able to see evidence of its validity in many aspects of life. Stated differently, we should be able to discover ways that a nonviolent Anabaptist perspective forms a comprehensive outlook with the potential to impact every aspect of life and thought. Or as John Howard Yoder once said,

> We cannot discuss theology alone, without interlocking with the human sciences which are talking about the same phenomena from other perspectives. If the believer says that faith in Jesus Christ makes love of the enemy imperative and possible, is this not something that could be described, and whose possibility could be measured, by the psychologist? If love leads someone to go out and make peace with one's adversary, is this not an event which a sociologist could describe? When a preacher proclaims that "Violence is always self-defeating," is that not a claim which the historian could verify or refute?[41]

A book on which we collaborated, along with other Bluffton faculty members, exemplifies the idea that any mode of inquiry and context of life should be subject to the story of Jesus. *Teaching Peace: Nonviolence and the Liberal Arts*[42] provides one example of such a comprehensive outlook. It has twenty-three chapters that show how nonviolence as a beginning principle has the potential to shape research or teaching in every discipline of the university curriculum. Some chapters contain surprises. A chapter on *actor training* exposes the intrinsic violence of "the method," the dominant theory of actor training.

Another chapter states that standard college textbooks in *psychology* discuss aggression and violence almost exclusively as problems of individuals. The failure of textbooks to discuss either the psychological factors that contribute to war or that belong to war's aftermath allows students to assume that war is so normal that there is no need to raise questions about it. Such textbooks provide few if any tools for thinking about the impact of war's violence on either its participants or its victims.

A chapter on *global marketization* exposes the structural violence against poorer countries that is inherent in the North American Free Trade Agreement (NAFTA). *Science* chapters on the human immune system and on primate behavior show that presuppositions about the givenness of violence in the paradigms scientists use to interpret data have a significant impact on how much violence scientists presume to find in nature. Chapters on *mathematics* use mathematical models to show that peace and nonviolence are logical and provide a number of examples to indicate that math is not a "neutral" discipline. How math is taught reflects prior assumptions about violence, nonviolence, and justice.

Beyond these brief examples, *Teaching Peace* has discussions on art, music, criminal justice, biblical interpretation, theology, literature, history, political science, communication, the professions and more. The intent of the book was to expand the places in which to recognize the presence of violence and then to visualize nonviolent alternatives. The Anabaptist story reminds us of discipleship, which makes rejection of violence integral to the Christian story. Such examples demonstrate that the nonviolent Anabaptist story does engender a comprehensive Christian orientation, a foretaste of the peaceable kingdom of God. From within the story of Jesus, one can begin truly to see the whole world.

DEFENSELESS CHRISTIANITY AND THE FUTURE

Nonviolent ecclesial Anabaptism as defenseless Christianity is a comprehensive perspective, an all-encompassing way to look at the world from the perspective of the crucified and resurrected Jesus. This was the situation for Anabaptists in the sixteenth century. It is the situation for Anabaptists in the twenty-first century. Contemporary Anabaptists are involved in the same task as their forebears in the sixteenth century. They are still trying to understand how to live in the tradition of nonviolent discipleship rooted in the comprehensive movement that continues the incarnation of Jesus known as the church. This movement carries on the mission of witnessing to the presence of the peaceable reign of God in the world.

We have an abstract understanding of the church shaped by the story of Jesus that rejects violence and that witnesses to the world from a stance of separation. But we are living in situations that the church has not lived in before. Out of the understanding of the story of Jesus, with a character formed by the story of Jesus, we live in these new situations by asking what the shape of the church is, what the posture of discipleship is in this new setting.

Elsewhere it was said that the church is always "becoming Anabaptist."[43] Or in the now familiar words of Hans Denck's dictim, "But the Means is Christ, whom none can truly know except he follow him with his life. And no one can follow him except insofar as one previously knows him."[44] There is no normative history that then also describes what the future is like. Rather there is a norm of faithfulness to the story of Jesus, against which every new move of the church is tested. The new moves may be different than anything that has come before and are worked out in the actually living out of the norm of the story of Jesus. Thus they cannot be fully predicted in advance.

In the twenty-first century, we—the church—face many new situations. Some come from changing social situations. How does the church witness against war and live in ways that do not contribute to war, in a nation where the economy is largely a war economy and simply buying the goods necessary for daily living immerses one in this military-based economy? How does modern warfare, with the advent of the belief that whole societies participate in the war effort, impact the Anabaptist peace church as its members become fully acculturated in contemporary society? How does the church address issues of gender and race discrimination, which are now outlawed by statute but still have significant societal manifestations accompanied by subtle defenses of the status quo?

Technology confronts us with a variety of health issues. There are debates about what constitutes human life as opposed to biological functioning and how to understand when life ends. One aspect concerns what has come to be called "stem cell research" and whether it destroys incipient human life. Another concerns when life ends for an individual for whom important bodily functions have ceased without possibility of recovery and remaining ones continue only with artificial support. Scientific research creates procedures and medications that clearly prolong life—but at costs that eliminate many people from benefiting from these advances and deprive others of even more basic health care. What are appropriate kinds of research, and how should health care be distributed and paid for? Is it appropriate, for example, to spend a million dollars on one premature infant who will require life-long adult care, when that amount of money would save the lives of many children if invested in vaccinations for infants in developing nations?

How do we live justly when most of the clothes we wear were manufactured in sweatshops outside of North America and much of our food and drink was produced in ways that did not benefit the local peasants who tended the crops? Should we make efforts to grow our own food and to buy only locally grown food products, which cuts down considerably on fuel costs of imports but requires much more time and effort we local consumers might otherwise invest in worthy service careers? In what way, if at all, are nonviolent Anabaptists responsible for security in the cities and towns where they live?

A previous section described the development of a new paradigm of atonement theology that would reflect the nonviolence of the Jesus narrative rather than the presumed violence of standard atonement theology. Since the development of that atonement paradigm, it has become increasingly clear, we believe, that much of standard theology presumes and/or accommodates some form of violence, either of God or by supposed disciples of Jesus. Thus development of nonviolence-shaped theology will continue.[45]

We rejoice at the increasing roles of women in leadership in our churches and in some areas of theology. Although in chapter one we noted the paucity of women in the historical conversation about the character of Anabaptism, women are better represented in some other areas of theology. Most Mennonite colleges, universities, and seminaries have at least one woman in the faculties of Bible or theology. A number of women contribute to the conversation about the contemporary character of Anabaptist theology through writing of literature and poetry and contemporary reflection and through regular columns in church periodicals.[46] Our own professional careers at Bluffton University were blessed by having a woman as our university president. This was the first time a woman had served as president of a Mennonite college or university. Similarly, our worship life in Bluffton was enriched by our lead pastor, the first woman to serve a large, traditional Mennonite congregation.

Nevertheless, some congregations remain reluctant to accept women as leaders, and women are still underrepresented in scholarly and leadership positions across our denomination and in many others. We ourselves need the critics who nudge us in our own treatment of Anabaptism adequately to engage the contributions of women. We believe that limiting the roles of women is an act of violence against the image of God that women bear. Advocating for women in positions of leadership thus needs to remain high on the agenda for the future of defenseless Christianity as nonviolent ecclesial Anabaptism. The same needs to be said for transforming the church into one that truly embraces people across ethnic and racial lines and makes it less likely that in the future a text like this one will be written by two white men.

In these and many more such areas, the church of nonviolent ecclesial Anabaptism as defenseless Christianity is finding its way ahead without knowing in advance exactly where it is going, just as surely as Anabaptists in the sixteenth-century were engaged in discovering what it meant to be the church separated from the world without having been there before. It is in the doing that it is discovered—we pray—what it means to be disciples of Jesus in these new situations.

We, as individuals and as a church, are finding our way forward without knowing exactly where we are going. But the single most important decision concerns whether we embrace the structures of the social order as the structures through which to carry out the mission to testify to the reign of God—or if we choose to see the church as the structure that witnesses most fundamentally to the reign of God in the world.

Anabaptism as defenseless Christianity makes clear that our primary loyalty is to the loving and gifted body of the Prince of Peace called the church. Whether or not we work in institutions of government, in business organizations or in other structures, our actions are to be guided by the life of discipleship—of living in the story of Jesus by the power of the Holy Spirit—just as much as if our pay checks came from a church institution. This is the meaning of nonviolent ecclesial Anabaptism and defenseless Christianity as a contemporary paradigm for the peace church.

NOTES

1. Harold S. Bender, *The Anabaptist Vision* (Scottdale, Pa.: Herald Press, 1944), 20.

2. John Howard Yoder, *The Politics of Jesus: Vicit Agnus Noster*, 2nd. ed. (Grand Rapids, Mich.: William B. Eerdmans, 1993), 5-8, 15-19.

3. John H. Yoder, "The Anabaptist Shape of Liberation," in *Why I Am a Mennonite: Essays on Mennonite Identity*, ed. Harry Loewen (Scottdale, Pa.: Herald Press, 1988), 339-43.

4. John H. Yoder, "Anabaptist Shape," 343-44.

5. Bender, *Anabaptist Vision*, 31.

6. John H. Yoder, "Anabaptist Shape," 339.

7. Hans Denck, *The Spiritual Legacy of Hans Denck: Interpretations and Translation of Key Texts*, interpreter and trans. Clarence Bauman, Studies in Medieval and Reformation Thought, vol. 47 (Leiden: E. J. Brill, 1991), 113.

8. Among the more recent of various such accounts is C. Arnold Snyder, "The Birth and Evolution of Swiss Anabaptism, 1520-1530," *The Mennonite Quarterly Review* 80, no. 4 (October 2006): 501-645.

9. A recent example of this application of supposed neutral observation to remove rejection of the sword as a "core trait" of first-generation Anabaptism is A. James Reimer, "Pacifism, Policing, and Individual Conscience," *The Conrad Grebel Review* 26, no. 2 (Spring 2008): 131.

10. A parallel description becoming normative occurs when contemporary theologians argue that sixteenth-century Anabaptist reference to and use of the classic creeds of Christendom prescribes modern use of those creeds for Mennonites. In contrast, the view of

dynamic Anabaptism presented in this essay has shown a willingness to revise and extend these classic creedal statements, as demonstrated in the section of Chapter 2 called "The Theological Novelty of Anabaptism as Defenseless Christianity" and extended in the section of this chapter called "Theology for Defenseless Christianity."

The move of a historical description becoming normative and/or ideological occurs in many instances. Another common one is the teaching about the Revolutionary War of 1776 in U.S. public schools. As this history is told, the war is the basis of freedom. This story then becomes the ideological justification—the proof—of the belief in the minds of many Americans that freedom depends on war. Other historical accounts, if known, would undercut this historical account. See for example, James C. Juhnke and Carol M. Hunter, *The Missing Peace: The Search for Nonviolent Alternatives in United States History*, 2nd ed. (Kitchener, Ont.: Pandora Press, 2004).

11. What is here informally called looping back, John Howard Yoder described as an ongoing "restitution," a "continuing series of new beginnings, similar in shape and spirit, as the objective historicity of Jesus and the apostles, mediated through the objectivity of scripture, encounters both the constants and the variables of every age to call forth 'restitutions' at once original and true-to-type, at once unpredictable and recognizable." John Howard Yoder, "Anabaptism and History," in *The Priestly Kingdom: Social Ethics as Gospel* (Notre Dame, Ind.: University of Notre Dame, 1984), 133.

12. Pilgram Marpeck, *The Writings of Pilgram Marpeck*, ed. and trans. William Klassen and Walter Klaassen, Classics of the Reformation, vol. 2 (Scottdale, Pa.: Herald Press, 1978), 423.

13. Gerald Biesecker-Mast, *Separation and the Sword in Anabaptist Persuasion: Radical Confessional Rhetoric from Schleitheim to Dordrecht*, The C. Henry Smith Series, vol. 6 (Telford, Pa.: Cascadia Publishing House, 2006; copublished Herald Press, 2006), 30-31.

14. Biesecker-Mast, *Separation and the Sword*, 97-108.

15. Author Weaver participated in three CPT teams to Haiti in 1992, 1993, 1995. For a report with biblical and theological analysis, see J. Denny Weaver, "Making Yahweh's Rule Visible," in *Peace and Justice Shall Embrace: Power and Theopolitics in the Bible: Essays in Honor of Millard Lind*, ed. Ted Grimsrud and Loren L. Johns (Telford, Pa.: Pandora Press U.S., 1999; copublished Herald Press, 1999), 34-48.

16. An example in Weaver's personal library is Martin Noth, *Geschichte Israels*, Sechste, unveränderte Auflage (Berlin: Evangelische Verlagsantalt, 1968).

17. John Howard Yoder, *Body Politics: Five Practices of the Christian Community Before the Watching World* (Scottdale, Pa.: Herald Press,

2001), ix.
18. John Howard Yoder, *Body Politics*, ch. 5.
19. John Howard Yoder, *Body Politics*, 33.
20. Jim S. Amstutz, *Threatened with Resurrection: Self-Preservation and Christ's Way of Peace* (Scottdale, Pa.: Herald Press, 2001).
21. Henry Funk, *A Mirror of Baptism with the Spirit, with Water and with Blood in Three Parts from the Holy Scriptures of the Old and New Testaments* (Mountain Valley, Va.: Joseph Funk and Sons, 1851).
22. Funk, *Mirror of Baptism*, 83.
23. Funk, *Mirror of Baptism*, 84.
24. Marpeck, *Writings of Marpeck*, 83.
25. The phrase "created and called for community" is borrowed from the theme of the inauguration of Kim Phipps as president of Messiah College on Friday, 14 October 2005.
26. Ephesians 5.18-20 TNIV and NRSV.
27. David F. Ford, *Self and Salvation* (Cambridge: Cambridge University Press, 1999; reprint 2003), 125.
28. Rowan Williams, *Why Study the Past? The Quest for the Historical Church* (Grand Rapids, Mich.: William B. Eerdmans Publishing Company, 2005), 92-93.
29. Williams, *Why Study*, 110.
30. Glen H. Stassen and Michael L. Westmoreland-White, "Defining Violence and Nonviolence," in *Teaching Peace: Nonviolence and the Liberal Arts*, ed. J. Denny Weaver and Gerald Biesecker-Mast (Lanham, Md.: Rowman & Littlefield Publishers, Inc., 2003), 18.
31. Funk, *Mirror of Baptism*, 83, 110.
32. Christian Burkholder, "Useful and Edifying Address to the Young, on True Repentance, Saving in Christ Jesus," in *Christian Spiritual Conversation on Saving Faith, for the Young, in Questions and Answers, and a Confession of Faith of the Mennonites, with an Appendix*, author and editor Gerrit Roosen, reprint, 1857 (Lancaster: John Baer and Sons, 1878), 211-17, quote 211. The German is Christian Burkholder, *Nützliche und Erbauliche Anrede an die Jugend, von der Wahren Buße Vom Seligmachenden Glauben an Christo Jesu, und der Reinen Liebe zu Gott und Seinem Nachsten; und dem Gehorsam der Worte Gottes und der Reinen Uebergabe der Seelen an Seine Hand*, 3rd. ed., reprint, 1804 (Allentown, Pa.: Heinrich Ebner & Comp., 1829), 31-35, quote 31.
33. J. Denny Weaver, *Keeping Salvation Ethical: Mennonite and Amish Atonement Theology in the Late Nineteenth Century*, foreword C. Norman Kraus, Studies in Anabaptist and Mennonite History (Scottdale, Pa.: Herald Press, 1997). For summaries of the argument of this book, see J. Denny Weaver, "Amish and Mennonite Soteriology: Revivalism and Free Church Theologizing in the Nineteenth-Century," *Fides et Historia* 27, no. 1 (Winter/Spring 1995): 30-52, and

his J. Denny Weaver, *Anabaptist Theology in Face of Postmodernity: A Proposal for the Third Millennium*, foreword by Glen Stassen, The C. Henry Smith Series, vol. 2 (Telford, Pa.: Pandora Press U.S., copublished Herald Press, 2000), 71-93.

34. J. Denny Weaver, *The Nonviolent Atonement* (Grand Rapids: Wm. B. Eerdmans Publishing Co., 2001). A revised and expanded edition of *The Nonviolent Atonement* is forthcoming. For summaries of the argument of this book, see J. Denny Weaver, "Violence in Christian Theology," *CrossCurrents* 51, no. 2 (Summer 2001): 150-76 , J. Denny Weaver, "Violence in Christian Theology," in *Cross Examinations: Readings on the Meaning of the Cross Today*, ed. Marit Trelstad (Minneapolis: Augsburg Fortress, 2006), 225-39, or J. Denny Weaver, "Atonement and (Non)violence," *The Epworth Review* 36, no. 1 (January 2009): 29-46.

35. For a definition of "standard theology," see note 45, chapter 2.

36. Neal Blough's recent assertion of the relevance the theology of Pilgram Marpeck and Anabaptism for the contemporary church reverses the order presented here. In other words, whereas our suggestion begins with the theology that emerges from the new ecclesiology of Anabaptism and shows how the issues of classic theology can be discussed within Anabaptist theology (as in producing narrative Christus Victor as a new image for the work of Christ), Blough wants to start with the trinitarian language and outline and then fill these entities with Anabaptist content. Neal Blough, *Christ in Our Midst: Incarnation, Church and Discipleship in the Theology of Pilgram Marpeck* (Kitchener, Ont.: Pandora Press, 2007), ch. 7. Here we indicate three problems with this approach. First, the trinitarian terminology of Trinity, Person, natures are not themselves biblical terms. Rather they are terms developed in later centuries to deal with what is found in the New Testament, namely how God relates to Jesus and to the Holy Spirit and Christ's Spirit and God's Spirit and so on in the multiple combinations in which they appear in the New Testament. We prefer to stay closer to the biblical outline.

Second, Blough appears to assume that the later trinitarian terminology along with its definitions are the only categories for expressing the meaning of the New Testament in later contexts. See Blough, *Christ in Our Midst*, 238-39. We agree fully that the classic terminology is a correct answer to the questions posed by the New Testament about the relationship of God and Christ and Spirit, if one wants the answer in terms of a fourth-century world view and its corresponding philosophical categories. However, these particular answers ought not be made universal ones. Our worldview differs from the fourth century, and other categories may provide appropriate answers to the New Testament questions in other contexts.

Finally, asserting the importance of classic theology in order to identify with the universal church while also redefining it in a particular Anabaptist way appears to pose an inevitable and unavoidable dilemma. Claiming common ground on the basis of redefined terminology will hardly satisfy the heirs of the just war tradition if it requires them to surrender their historic support of war and national defense. Besides it is hardly common ground if each side has different understandings.

On the other hand, one can also use the classic language, with Anabaptist discipleship to the particular story of Jesus, nonviolence, voluntary church, and more as particular additions to the meaning of the classic language. But in this case, discipleship to Jesus and nonviolence are no longer intrinsic to a commitment to Jesus, as Anabaptism represented by Marpeck would claim. For further discussion of the difference between ecumenical conversations that focus on agreements versus differences, see John Howard Yoder, "On Christian Unity: The Way from Below," *Pro Ecclesia* 9, no. 2 (Spring 2001): 165-83. Thomas Finger presents a quite extended version of using classic language redefined with Anabaptist content. See his *A Contemporary Anabaptist Theology: Biblical, Historical, Constructive* (Downers Grove, Ill.: InterVarsity Press, 2004). For Weaver's critique of this methodology, see J. Denny Weaver, "Parsing Anabaptist Theology: A Review Essay of Thomas N. Finger's *A Contemporary Anabaptist Theology*," *Direction* 34, no. 2 (Fall 2005): 241-63.

37. John Howard Yoder, *The Priestly Kingdom: Social Ethics as Gospel* (Notre Dame, Ind.: University of Notre Dame Press, 1984), 4-5.

38. John L. Ruth, *Maintaining the Right Fellowship: A Narrative Account of Life in the Oldest Mennonite Community in North America*, Studies in Anabaptist and Mennonite History, no. 26 (Scottdale, Pa.: Herald Press, 1984), 343-456.

39. For description and analysis of these and other changes, see Theron F. Schlabach, *Gospel Versus Gospel: Mission and the Mennonite Church, 1863-1944*, Studies in Anabaptist and Mennonite History, no. 21 (Scottdale, Pa.: Herald Press, 1980); Theron F. Schlabach, *Peace, Faith, Nation: Mennonites and Amish in Nineteenth-Century America*, The Mennonite Experience in America, vol. 2 (Scottdale, Pa.: Herald, 1988); and James C. Juhnke, *Vision, Doctrine, War: Mennonite Identity and Organization in America 1890-1930*, Mennonite Experience in America, vol. 3 (Scottdale, Pa.: Herald Press, 1989).

40. Jason Moyer, "The Confessional Atheism of Policy Governance: Freeing the Church to Articulate God's Logos," For the Consultation, Holding Fast to the Confession of Our Hope: The Confession of Faith Ten Years Later (Associated Mennonite Biblical Seminaries, 2006). Copy of paper in possession of Gerald Mast.

41. John Howard Yoder, "The Science of Conflict," Lecture no. 5 in the Warsaw series (Warsaw, Poland, 1983), 1. Our thanks to Mark Thiessen Nation, who supplied a copy of the lecture from the Yoder Collection at Eastern Mennonite Seminary.

42. J. Denny Weaver and Gerald Biesecker-Mast, eds., *Teaching Peace: Nonviolence and the Liberal Arts* (Lanham, Md.: Rowman & Littlefield Publishers, Inc., 2003).

43. See the title and quote of J. Denny Weaver, *Becoming Anabaptist: The Origin and Significance of Sixteenth-Century Anabaptism*, 2nd ed., foreword by William H. Willimon (Scottdale, Pa.: Herald Press, 2005), 222.

44. Denck, *Spiritual Legacy*, 113.

45. For initial conversation on the nonviolence of God, see J. Denny Weaver, "God in the Dock: Challenging Images of Divine Violence," The C. Henry Smith Peace Lecture, presented at Bluffton University and Goshen College in Spring 2006 and at the General Assembly of Mennonite Church USA, in San Jose, California, July 2007, and a longer, three-part version: "The Nonviolent God: I: Common Understandings of God as Violent; II: The Hebrew Experience; III: Is the Revelator's God Violent?" at Portland Mennonite Church, Portland, Oregon, April 2007. For an initial response to the intrinsic violence of two-kingdom theology, see J. Denny Weaver, "Living in the Reign of God in the 'Real World': Getting Beyond Two-Kingdom Theology," in *Exiles in the Empire: Believers Church Perspectives on Politics*, ed. Nathan E. Yoder and Carol A. Scheppard, Studies in the Believers Church Tradition (Kitchener, Ont.: Pandora Press, 2006), 173-93.

46. Following is a very select list of titles. In addition to her books of poetry, see Julia Kasdorf, *The Body and the Book: Writing from a Mennonite Life* (Baltimore: Johns Hopkins Press, 2001); Melanie May, *A Body Knows: A Theopoetics of Death and Resurrection* (New York: Continuum, 1995); Nancey Murphy, *Reconciling Theology and Science: A Radical Reformation Perspective* (Kitchener, Ont.: Pandora Press, 1997); Sara Wenger Shenk, *Anabaptist Ways of Knowing: A Conversation About Tradition-Based Critical Education* (Telford, Pa.: Cascadia Publishing House, 2003; copublished Herald Press, 2003); Sara Wenger Shenk and Deborah Good, eds., *Thank You for Asking: Conversing With Young Adults About the Future Church* (Scottdale, Pa.: Herald Press, 2005); Katie Funk Wiebe, *You Never Gave Me a Name: One Mennonite Woman's Story* (Telford, Pa.: Dreamseeker Books/ Cascadia, 2009; copublished Herald Press, 2009), in which Wiebe, born into early twentieth-century socialization of women as mothers, homemakers, and supportive wives, traces her own experience as a woman gaining a public voice against daunting odds.

Appendix: On the So-Called Paradigmatic "Void" in Anabaptist Studies

IN A RECENT SURVEY OF Radical Reformation scholarship, R. Emmett McLaughlin laments the retirement of the generation of revisionist Anabaptist scholars that "put Anabaptism on the Reformation map," and made Anabaptist studies respectable in the academy by removing the taint of confessional bias through what he describes as a successful "assault" on The Anabaptist Vision of Harold Bender, an assault he says took place primarily through the vehicle of social history.[1] The retirement of the leaders of the revisionist assault, according to McLaughlin, "changes the landscape dramatically and leaves a void that may not be filled." Furthermore, as he states: "Without the intellectual energy and academic respectability that social history provided, not to mention the close relationship to the Peasants' War that reconnected Anabaptism with the larger society, there is a real danger that the field will become again an historical backwater in which justifiable Mennonite concerns for identity and faith will overshadow the historians' commitment to understand the past, warts and all."[3]

No doubt this book fits rather well into the historical backwater McLaughlin imagines, since it is based to a significant extent on the concerns of the contemporary church and seeks to identify with those forms of Anabaptism that can help the church in twenty-first century faithfulness. We imagine that it might also resemble what James Stayer has termed an "anti-secularist" reaction in Anabaptist studies, insofar as it uses theological concern as a point of departure for examining historical texts.[4]

However, we propose that our telling of the story of Anabaptism is best seen as what Jean-Francois Lyotard called a *petite narrative* shaped by a petite paradigm in a field of study that can no longer expect a grand narrative or a single big paradigm to either assault or be assaulted by. A study of defenseless Anabaptist theological rhetoric from the perspective of "confessional history" offers one more way to think about the meaning of Anabaptism amid a proliferation of paradigms. That a proliferation of paradigms appears as an emerging void may have more to do with whether one's own, once dominant paradigm now has to compete with other paradigms than with the appearance of an actual void.

Our study of Anabaptist theology and rhetoric seeks to be honest about the kind of curiosity by which it is motivated: What can Anabaptist history and theology teach us about the faithful articulation of the gospel of Jesus Christ as a gospel of peace? It takes seriously the contentious nature of both early Anabaptist texts and contemporary analysis of such texts by highlighting the conflicts the text address and by offering a critical assessment of past efforts to account for Anabaptist defenselessness. It does not assume the need to speak a secular or neutral methodological language to be coherent across disciplines. If this approach exhibits a methodological innovation, it is this: Anabaptist texts are understood not so much as ideas with precedents nor as ideologies with a social origin—but as competing embodied arguments, each with a story that includes both a genealogy and an exigence.

We hope that our interest in finding a usable past for Anabaptist-identified churches today can be useful not only to the church but to all those curious about the origins and characteristics of sixteenth-century Christian radicalism. We have learned much from historians who place Anabaptist movements in relationship to social realities other than the church. We hope that others learn from our perspective on the past, and we welcome a vigorous conversation from all quarters about the meaning and significance of Anabaptism. We anticipate an expanded conversation, in other words, rather than a "void."

NOTES

1. R. Emmet McLaughlin, "Radicals," in *Reformation and Early Modern Europe: A Guide to Research*, ed. David M. Whitford (Kirksville, Mo.: Truman State University Press, 2008), 105, 109.

2. McLaughlin, "Radicals," 109-10.

3. Two papers from Stayer for the Anabaptist colloquium lament the "anti-secularist" turn in Anabaptist studies. These papers are available in the Mennonite Historical Library at Goshen College.

Bibliography

Amstutz, Jim S. *Threatened with Resurrection: Self-Preservation and Christ's Way of Peace*. Scottdale, Pa.: Herald Press, 2001.

Bartlett, Anthony W. *Cross Purposes: The Violent Grammar of Christian Atonement*. Harrisburg, Pa.: Trinity Press International, 2001.

Bender, Harold S. "The Anabaptist Vision." *Church History* 13, no. 1 (March 1944): 3-24.

―――. *The Anabaptist Vision*. Scottdale, Pa.: Herald Press, 1944.

―――. "The Anabaptist Vision." *Mennonite Quarterly Review* 18, no. 2 (April 1944): 67-88.

―――. "The Anabaptist Vision." In *The Recovery of the Anabaptist Vision: A Sixtieth Anniversary Tribute to Harold S. Bender*, ed. Guy F. Hershberger, 29-54. Scottdale, Pa.: Herald Press, 1970.

Biesecker-Mast, Gerald. "Critique and Subjection in Anabaptist Political Witness." In *Exiles in the Empire: Believers Church Perspectives on Politics*, ed. Nathan E. Yoder and Carol A. Scheppard. Studies in the Believers Church Tradition, 45-59. Kitchener, Ont.: Pandora Press, 2006.

―――. "Response to Snyder." *The Mennonite Quarterly Review* 80, no. 4 (October 2006): 651-57.

―――. *Separation and the Sword in Anabaptist Persuasion: Radical Confessional Rhetoric from Schleitheim to Dordrecht*. The C. Henry Smith Series, vol. 6. Telford, Pa.: Cascadia Publishing House, 2006.

Blough, Neal. *Christ in Our Midst: Incarnation, Church and Discipleship in the Theology of Pilgram Marpeck*. Kitchener, Ont.: Pandora Press, 2007.

―――. "Pilgram Marpeck, Martin Luther and the Humanity of Christ." *Mennonite Quarterly Review* 61, no. 2 (April 1987): 203-12.

Brock, Rita Nakashima. *Journeys by Heart: A Christology of Erotic Power*. New York: Crossroad, 1991.

――― and Rebecca Ann Parker. *Saving Paradise: How Christianity Traded Love of This World for Crucifixion and Empire*. Boston: Beacon Press, 2008.

Brown, Joanne Carlson and Carole R. Bohn, eds. *Christianity, Patriarchy, and Abuse: A Feminist Critique.* New York: The Pilgrim Press, 1989.

Brueggemann, Walter. *The Theology of the Old Testament: Testimony, Dispute, Advocacy.* Minneapolis: Fortress Press, 1997.

Burkholder, Christian. *Nützliche und Erbauliche Anrede an die Jugend, von der Wahren Buße Vom Seligmachenden Glauben an Christo Jesu, und der Reinen Liebe zu Gott und Seinem Nachsten; und dem Gehorsam der Worte Gottes und der Reinen Uebergabe der Seelen an Seine Hand.* 3rd ed. 1804. Allentown, Pa.: Heinrich Ebner & Comp., 1829.

———. "Useful and Edifying Address to the Young, on True Repentance, Saving in Christ Jesus." In *Christian Spiritual Conversation on Saving Faith, for the Young, in Questions and Answers, and a Confession of Faith of the Mennonites, with an Appendix,* author and editor Gerrit Roosen. 1857, 179-257. Lancaster: John Baer and Sons, 1878.

The Chronicle of the Hutterian Brethren, vol. 1. Edited and trans. Hutterian Brethren. Rifton, N.Y.: Plough Publishing House, 1987.

de Certeau, Michel. *The Practice of Everyday Life.* Berkeley: University of California Press, 1984.

Cone, James H. *God of the Oppressed,* rev. ed. Maryknoll, N.Y.: Orbis Books, 1997.

Denck, Hans. *The Spiritual Legacy of Hans Denck: Interpretations and Translation of Key Texts.* Interpreter and trans. Clarence Bauman. Studies in Medieval and Reformation Thought, vol. 47. Leiden: E. J. Brill, 1991.

Dyck, Cornelius J., William E. Keeney, and Alvin Beachy, trans. and eds. *The Writings of Dirk Philips 1504-1568.* Classics of the Radical Reformation, vol. 6. Scottdale, Pa.: Herald Press, 1992.

Finger, Thomas. "Confessions of Faith in the Anabaptist/Mennonite Tradition." *The Mennonite Quarterly Review* 76, no. 3 (July 2002): 277-97.

———. "Response to Snyder." *The Mennonite Quarterly Review* 80, no. 4 (October 2006): 660-66.

Finger, Tom. "Pilgram Marpeck and the Christus Victor Motif." *The Mennonite Quarterly Review* 78, no. 1 (January 2004): 53-78.

Ford, David F. *Self and Salvation.* Cambridge: Cambridge University Press, 1999; reprint 2003.

Friesen, Abraham. *Erasmus, the Anabaptists, and the Great Commission.* Grand Rapids, Mich.: William B. Eerdmans Publishing Co., 1988.

Friesen, John J., trans. and ed. *Peter Riedemann's Hutterite Confessions of Faith.* Classics of the Radical Reformation, vol. 9. Scottdale, Pa.: Herald Press, 1999.

Funk, Henry. *A Mirror of Baptism with the Spirit, with Water and with Blood in Three Parts from the Holy Scriptures of the Old and New Testaments.* Mountain Valley, Va.: Joseph Funk and Sons, 1851.

Gingerich, Ray. "The Canons of Anabaptism: Which Anabaptism? Whose Canon?" In *The Work of Jesus Christ in Anabaptist Perspective: Essays in Honor of J. Denny Weaver,* ed. Alain Epp Weaver and Gerald J. Mast, 191-222. Telford, Pa.: Cascadia Publishing House; copublished Herald Press, 2008.

———. "Response to Snyder." *The Mennonite Quarterly Review* 80, no. 4 (October 2006): 670-74.

Harder, Leland, ed. *The Sources of Swiss Anabaptism: The Grebel Letters and Related Documents.* Classics of the Radical Reformation, vol. 4. Scottdale, Pa.: Herald Press, 1985.

Juhnke, James C. *Vision, Doctrine, War: Mennonite Identity and Organization in America 1890-1930.* Mennonite Experience in America, vol. 3. Scottdale, Pa.: Herald Press, 1989.

———., and Carol M. Hunter. *The Missing Peace: The Search for Nonviolent Alternatives in United States History.* Second Expanded ed. Kitchner, Ont.: Pandora Press.

Kasdorf, Julia. *The Body and the Book: Writing from a Mennonite Life.* Baltimore: Johns Hopkins Press, 2001.Keeney, William. "The Incarnation, a Central Theological Concept." In *A Legacy of Faith: The Heritage of Menno Simons: Sixtieth Anniversary Tribute to Cornelius Krahn,* ed. Cornelius J. Dyck. Mennonite Historical Series, vol. 8, 55-68. Newton, Kan.: Faith and Life Press, 1962.

Marpeck, Pilgram. *The Writings of Pilgram Marpeck.* Ed. and trans. William Klassen and Walter Klaassen. Classics of the Reformation. Scottdale, Pa.: Herald Press, 1978.

Mast, Gerald J. "Jesus' Flesh and the Faithful Church in the Theological Rhetoric of Menno Simons." In *The Work of Jesus Christ in Anabaptist Perspective: Essays in Honor of J. Denny Weaver,* ed. Alain Epp Weaver and Gerald J. Mast, 173-90. Telford, Pa.: Cascadia Publishing House; copublished Herald Press, 2008.

May, Melanie. *A Body Knows: A Theopoetics of Death and Resurrection.* New York: Continuum, 1995.

McLaren, Brian D. *A Generous Orthodoxy: Why I Am a Missional, Evangelical, Post-Protestant, Liberal/Conservative, Mystical/- Poetic, Biblical, Charismatic/Contemplative, Fundamentalist/- Calvinist, Anabaptist/Anglican, Methodist, Catholic, Green, Incarnational, Depressed-Yet-Hopeful, Emergent, Unfinished Christian.* Grand Rapids, Mich.: Zondervan, 2004.

McLaughlin, R. Emmet. "Radicals." In *Reformation and Early Modern Europe: A Guide to Research*, ed. David M. Whitford, 80-120. Kirksville, Mo.: Truman State University Press, 2008.

Menno Simons. *The Complete Writings of Menno Simons c.1496-1561.* Ed. John Christian Wenger. Trans. Leonard Verduin, with biography by Harold S. Bender. Scottdale, Pa.: Herald Press, 1956.

Moyer, Jason. "The Confessional Atheism of Policy Governance: Freeing the Church to Articulate God's Logos." For the Consultation, Holding Fast to the Confession of Our Hope: The Confession of Faith Ten Years Later. Associated Mennonite Biblical Seminaries, 2006.

Murphy, Nancey. *Reconciling Theology and Science: A Radical Reformation Perspective.* Kitchener, Ont.: Pandora Press, 1997.

Noth, Martin. *Geschichte Israels.* Sechste, unveränderte Auflage. Berlin: Evangelische Verlagsantalt, 1968.

Packull, Werner O. *Hutterite Beginnings: Communitarian Experiments During the Reformation.* Baltimore, Md.: The John Hopkins University Press, 1995.

Reimer, A. James. "Pacifism, Policing, and Individual Conscience." *The Conrad Grebel Review* 26, no. 2 (Spring 2008): 129-41.

Rhodes, Robert. "National Identity Focus of Resolution." *Mennonite Weekly Review*, 2007, 16 July 2007, 6-7.

Riall, Robert A., trans., Galen A. Peters, ed. *The Earliest Hymns of the Ausbund: Some Beautiful Christian Songs Composed and Sung in the Prison at Passau, Published in 1564.* Anabaptist Texts in Translation. Kitchener, Ont.: Pandora Press, 2003.

Ruether, Rosemary Radford. *Sexism and God-Talk: Toward a Feminist Theology.* Boston: Beacon Press, 1983.

Ruth, John L. *Maintaining the Right Fellowship: A Narrative Account of Life in the Oldest Mennonite Community in North America.* Studies in Anabaptist and Mennonite History, vol. 26. Scottdale, Pa.: Herald Press, 1984.

Schlabach, Theron F. *Gospel Versus Gospel: Mission and the Mennonite Church, 1863-1944.* Studies in Anabaptist and Mennonite History, vol. 21. Scottdale, Pa.: Herald Press, 1980.

————. *Peace, Faith, Nation: Mennonites and Amish in Nineteenth-Century America.* The Mennonite Experience in America, vol. 2. Scottdale, Pa.: Herald, 1988.

Shenk, Sara Wenger. *Anabaptist Ways of Knowing: A Conversation About Tradition-Based Critical Educationg.* Telford, Pa.: Cascadia Publishing House, 2003; copublished Herald Press., 2003.

Shenk, Sara Wenger and Deborah Good, eds. *Thank You For Asking: Conversing With Young Adults About the Future Church.* Scottdale, Pa.: Herald Press, 2005.

Smith, C. Henry. *Mennonites in History.* Scottdale, Pa.: Mennnonite Book and Tract Society, 1907.

Snyder, C. Arnold. *Anabaptist History and Theology: An Introduction.* Kitchener, Ont.: Pandora Press, 1995.

————. "Beyond Polygenesis: Recovering the Unity and Diversity of Anabaptist Theology." In *Essays in Anabaptist Theology*, ed. H. Wayne Pipkin. Text Reader Series, 1-34. Elkhart, Ind.: Institute of Mennonite Studies, 1994.

————. "The Birth and Evolution of Swiss Anabaptism, 1520-1530." *The Mennonite Quarterly Review* 80, no. 4 (October 2006): 501-645.

————. *Following in the Footsteps of Christ: The Anabaptist Tradition.* Ed. Philip Sheldrake. Traditions of Christian Spirituality. Maryknoll, N.Y.: Orbis Books, 2004.

————. *From Anabaptist Seed: The Historical Core of Anabaptist-Related Identity.* Kitchener, Ont.: Pandora Press, 1999.

————. "Signposts of Faith." *Leader* 6, no. 1 (Fall 2008): 2-4.

Snyder, C. Arnold and Linda A. Huebert Hecht, eds. *Profiles of Anabaptist Women: Sixteenth-Century Reforming Pioneers,* Studies in Women and Religion/Études sur les femmes et la religion, vol. 3. Waterloo, Ont.: Published for the Canadian Cooperation for Studies in Religion by Wilfrid Laurier University Press, 1996.

Sprunger, Keith L. "Printing 'Not So Necessary': Dutch Anabaptists and the Telling of Martyr Stories." *The Mennonite Quarterly Review* 80, no. 2 (April 2006): 149-84.

Stassen, Glen H., and Michael L. Westmoreland-White. "Defining Violence and Nonviolence." In *Teaching Peace: Nonviolence and the Liberal Arts*, ed. J. Denny Weaver and Gerald Biesecker-Mast, 17-36. Lanham, Md.: Rowman & Littlefield Publishers, Inc., 2003.

Stayer, James M. *Anabaptists and the Sword.* Lawrence: Coronado Press, 1972.

————. *The German Peasants' War and the Anabaptist Community of Goods.* McGill-Queen's Studies in the History of Religion, vol. 6. Montreal & Kingston: McGill-Queen's University Press, 1991.

Stayer, James M., Werner O. Packull, and Klaus Deppermann. "From Monogenesis to Polygenesis: The Historical Discussion of Anabaptist Origins." *Mennonite Quarterly Review* 49, no. 2 (April 1975): 83-122.

Thistlethwaite, Susan Brooks. *Sex, Race and God: Christian Feminism in Black and White.* New York: Crossroad, 1991.

van Braght, Thieleman J. *The Bloody Theater or Martyrs Mirror of the Defenseless Christians Who Baptized Only Upon Confession of Faith, and Who Suffered and Died for the Testimony of Jesus, Their Savior, from the Time of Christ to the Year A.D. 1660.* Trans. Joseph F. Sohm. Scottdale, Pa.: Mennonite Publishing House, 1950.

Weaver, J. Denny. "Amish and Mennonite Soteriology: Revivalism and Free Church Theologizing in the Nineteenth-Century." *Fides et Historia* 27, no. 1 (Winter/Spring 1995): 30-52.

————. "Atonement and (Non)violence." *The Epworth Review* 36, no. 1 (January 2009):29-46.

————. *Anabaptist Theology in Face of Postmodernity: A Proposal for the Third Millennium.* With a foreword by Glen Stassen. The C. Henry Smith Series, vol. 2. Telford, Pa.: Pandora Press U.S.; copublished Herald Press, 2000.

————. *Becoming Anabaptist: The Origin and Significance of Sixteenth-Century Anabaptism.* Scottdale, Pa.: Herald Press, 1987.

————. *Becoming Anabaptist: The Origin and Significance of Sixteenth-Century Anabaptism.* 2nd ed. With a foreword by William H. Willimon. Scottdale, Pa.: Herald Press, 2005.

————. "Hubmaier Versus Hut on the Work of Christ: The Fifth Nicolsburg Article." *Archiv Für Reformationsgeschichte* 82 (1991): 171-92.

————. *Keeping Salvation Ethical: Mennonite and Amish Atonement Theology in the Late Nineteenth Century.* Foreword C. Norman Kraus. Studies in Anabaptist and Mennonite History. Scottdale, Pa.: Herald Press, 1997.

————. "Living in the Reign of God in the 'Real World': Getting Beyond Two-Kingdom Theology." In *Exiles in the Empire: Believers Church Perspectives on Politics,* ed. Nathan E. Yoder and Carol A. Scheppard. Studies in the Believers Church Tradition, 173-93. Kitchener, Ont.: Pandora Press, 2006.

————. "Making Yahweh's Rule Visible." In *Peace and Justice Shall Embrace: Power and Theopolitics in the Bible: Essays in Honor of Millard Lind*, ed. Ted Grimsrud and Loren L. Johns, 34-48. Telford, Pa.: Pandora Press, 1999; copublished Herald Press, 1999

————. *The Nonviolent Atonement*. Grand Rapids: Wm. B. Eerdmans Publishing Co., 2001.

————. "Response to Snyder." *The Mennonite Quarterly Review* 80, no. 4 (October 2006): 685-90.

————. "Violence in Christian Theology." *CrossCurrents* 51, no. 2 (Summer 2001): 150-76.

————. "Violence in Christian Theology." In *Cross Examinations: Readings on the Meaning of the Cross Today*, ed. Marit Trelstad, 225-39. Minneapolis: Augsburg Fortress, 2006.

————. "The Work of Christ: On the Difficulty of Identifying an Anabaptist Perspective." *Mennonite Quarterly Review* 59, no. 2 (April 1985): 107-29.

———— and Gerald Biesecker-Mast, eds. *Teaching Peace: Nonviolence and the Liberal Arts*. Lanham, Md.: Rowman & Littlefield Publishers, Inc., 2003.

Wiebe, Katie Funk. *You Never Gave Me a Name: One Mennonite Woman's Story*. Telford, Pa.: Dreamseeker Books, 2009.

Williams, Delores S. *Sisters in the Wilderness: The Challenge of Womanist God-Talk*. Maryknoll, N.Y.: Orbis Books, 1993.

Williams, Rowan. *Why Study the Past? The Quest for the Historical Church*. Grand Rapids, Mich.: William B. Eerdmans Publishing Company, 2005.

Yoder, John Howard, "The Anabaptist Shape of Liberation." In *Why I Am a Mennonite: Essays on Mennonite Identity*, ed. Harry Loewen, 338-48. Scottdale, Pa.: Herald Press, 1988.

————. "Armaments and Eschatology." *Studies in Christian Ethics* 1 (1988): 43-61.

————. *Body Politics: Five Practices of the Christian Community Before the Watching World*. Scottdale, Pa.: Herald Press, 2001.

————. trans. and ed. *The Legacy of Michael Sattler*. Classics of the Radical Reformation, vol. 1. Scottdale, Pa.: Herald Press, 1973.

————. *The Politics of Jesus: Vicit Agnus Noster*. 2nd. ed. Grand Rapids, Mich.: William B. Eerdmans, 1993.

————. *The Priestly Kingdom: Social Ethics as Gospel*. Notre Dame, Ind.: University of Notre Dame Press, 1984.

————. "The Science of Conflict." Lecture no. 5 in the Warsaw series. Warsaw, Poland, 1983.

The Index

"Little Flock," 40, 42
Normativity of Jesus, 58,
    62, 74, 76
Peace churches, 23-24, 43,
    72, 80
Priestly, 91-92
of Jesus Christ, 16, 17, 20,
    36, 40, 72
Separated, 30-33, 36-37, 40,
    49, 58-59, 81-84, 100
Source of truth, 85-86
Structures, 102-107
Theology, 45-57, 94-102
Theory and practice, 43, 74-
    75, 78, 84, 92-94, 103-104
"without spot or wrinkle,"
    36
As Witness, 24-25, 31, 36,
    59, 62-63, 77, 79, 81, 84,
    89, 91-94, 97-99, 105-107,
    111
Civil Authorities, 29, 33-37, 59-
    62, 82, 106
Civil Rights Movement, 65n9
Community, 91
    Church, 90-91
    Faith, 94
Cullman, Oscar, 15

D
Damascus Road, 87
de Certeau, Michel, 65n9
Defenseless Christianity,
    Always becoming, 108-111
    As Anabaptism, 23-30, 72-
        81
    As ecclesiology, 40-45, 62,
        65n12
    Dutch, 35-36
    For all Christians, 23, 25
    Nonviolence, 92-94
    And structures, 102-107
    Swiss, 31-34

South German, 34-35
Theological novelty, 45-57,
    67n46, 995-102, 112n10
    As worldview, 107-108
Defenselessness, 15, 34
    Anabaptist, 76, 78, 81-82,
        91, 93, 100, 104, 118
    Christ, 81
    Christianity, 23-29, 60, 62,
        72, 75-78, 81, 85, 92-95,
        100-111
    Church, 40
    Community, 77
    Life, 87
    Separation, 36
Denck, Hans, 37, 45, 79, 109
de Ries, Hans, 53
Deutsche Democratische Re-
    publik [DDR], 83
Dirk Philips, 43-44, 74
Discipleship. See also *Anabap-
    tism, as Discipleship*
    As ecclesiology, 73-79
    As nonviolence, 57, 70n72,
        108-109
    As practice, 84-93, 111
    And theology, 45-52, 55, 95-
        102, 110
Dutch Mennonite Confessions,
    52-55
    Flemish, 52
    Frisian, 52
    Upper German, 52
Dutch Russian, 96
Doctrine, 53

E
Ecclesiology, 28, 54, 62, 74, 100
    See also *Church*
    Anabaptist, 31, 33, 40, 45,
        51-52, 56-59, 61, 74, 76,
        79, 95, 98
    Christus Victor, 101

St. Paul, Minnesota, 25
Stendahl, Krister, 15
Suffering, 44, 50-51, 68n53, 87-88, 95-96, 99
Swiss Anabaptist, 96
Swiss Brethren, 40-41
Switzerland, 36
Sword, 58, 56, 74, 82
Rejection of, 34, 39, 47-48, 57, 59, 61

T
Teaching Peace, Nonviolence and the Liberal Arts, 107-108
Technology, 110
Theology,
Anabaptist, 45-57, 61, 86, 94-102, 110, 119
Atonement, 46-48, 95-99, 110
Chalcedonian, 48-50, 55
Trinitarian, 46, 50, 52, 100, 115n36
Tithe, 31-32
Trinity. See *God, Trinitarian*
Truth, 85, 91
Church, 85
Norm, 74
Twisck, Peter Jansz, 53

U
United Kingdom, 25
United States, 82, 93-94

V
Valerius, 46
Violence, 28, 44, 59, 77, 80, 82, 92-94, 109
Addressed by the Gospel, 16, 20, 23, 77
Defined, 92-94, 101, 107-108
Faith in, 77, 82, 84

In theology, 96, 110
Redemptive, 72
Rejection of, 23, 28, 38, 40, 48, 59, 75-77, 86-87, 109-110
"Respectable," 82
Self-defeating, 107
Structural and Systemic, 92-94
von Freyburg, Helena, 63

W
Waldeck, Franz von (Prince-Bishop of Münster), 35
Waldshut, 32
Weaver, J. Denny, 25, 95
Becoming Anabaptist, 26
Keeping Salvation Ethical, 96
Nonviolence Atonement, The, 97
Teaching Peace, 26
Westmoreland-White, Michael,
Teaching Peace, 92
Williams, Rowan, 20, 90
Women, 16, 20-21, 63, 94, 99, 101, 110-111

Y
Yahweh, 106
Yoder, John Howard, 23, 75-76, 84, 101-102, 107, 113n11
Body Politics, 84, 86
The Politics of Jesus, 15-16, 18, 74

Z
Zollikon, 32-33
Zurich, Switzerland, 26, 31-33, 36
Zwingli, Ulrich, 32

The Authors

GERALD J. MAST IS PROFESSOR OF COMMUNICATION at Bluffton University. He is the author of *Separation and the Sword in Anabaptist Persuasion* (2006) and co-editor of numerous books, including *Teaching Peace: Nonviolence and the Liberal Arts* (2003) and *The Work of Jesus Christ in Anabaptist Perspective* (2008). A graduate of Malone College, he received a Ph.D. in rhetoric and communication from the University of Pittsburgh.

Mast was born and raised in Holmes County, Ohio, with deep family roots in the Amish and conservative Mennonite communities. Throughout his life, he has remained affiliated with the Mennonite church and is presently a member of First Mennonite Church, Bluffton, Ohio. He currently serves as the vice-chair of *The Mennonite* magazine board and as editor of Studies in Anabaptist and Mennonite History.

Mast is married to Carrie (Roth) Mast and is the father of two young children, Anna and Jacob.

J. DENNY WEAVER IS PROFESSOR EMERITUS OF RELIGION and the Harry and Jean Yoder Scholar in Bible and Religion of Bluffton University where he taught for thirty-one years. He also taught one year at Goshen College (1974-75) and was Visiting Professor of Theology at Canadian Mennonite Bible College (1990-91). He is editor of The C. Henry Smith Series, which contains 9 volumes to date, with several others in process. His first book was the first edition of *Becoming Anabaptist* (1987). Since then he has written *Keeping Salvation Ethical* (1997), *Anabaptist Theology in Face of Postmodernity* (2000), *The Nonviolent Atonement* (2001), co-edited *Teaching Peace: Nonviolence and the Liberal*

Arts (2003), and produced a revised. second edition of *Becoming Anabaptist* (2005). He has also written numerous articles and book chapters on issues of peace theology, Anabaptist theology, Christology, and atonement.

Although retired from teaching, Weaver remains active in speaking and writing. A primary focus of his work is to show how a beginning assumption of nonviolence rooted in the story of Jesus has the potential to shape the formation of any theological issue and to impact the way history is written. This work has stirred significant interest in academic and church settings both in and beyond the historic peace churches. He is a frequent speaker in a variety of church and academic settings, for both popular and academic audiences. He has lectured in the United Kingdom and taught during short terms in Kenya and the Congo.

Weaver was born and raised at the edge of Kansas City, Kansas. The family attended the Argentine Mennonite church, which he joined at a young age. He has had a lifelong involvement with the Mennonite church and now belongs to Madison Mennonite Church in Madison, Wisconsin, where he moved after retiring from teaching. He attended Hesston College, and graduated from Goshen College with a major in mathematics. Following two years at Associated Mennonite Biblical Seminary, he volunteered with Mennonite Central Committee for conscientious objector service during the Vietnam War.

He and his wife had a year of French language instruction in Belgium and France, and then Weaver taught English as a second language for two years in a public Lycée in Algeria under MCC's Teachers Abroad Program. He then spent a year in Germany learning German and studying at a German seminary. Following these four years abroad, Weaver finished seminary at AMBS, and earned a Ph.D. in church history from Duke University. In the 1990s he served with three different Christian Peacemaker Teams delegations in Haiti.

Weaver is married to Mary Lois (Wenger) Weaver. They have three adult daughters, four grandsons, and two granddaughters.

Breinigsville, PA USA
07 October 2009
225407BV00001B/10/P